3 1397 00019 0820

D1401318

The Picture Framer's Handbook

The Picture Framer's Handbook

The Other Artist

Laurence & Janet Burnett

Photographs by Stan Rosol

 Clarkson N. Potter, Inc./Publisher   NEW YORK

DISTRIBUTED BY CROWN PUBLISHERS, INC.

Published simultaneously in Canada by General Publishing
Company Limited.
Inquiries should be addressed to Clarkson N. Potter, Inc.,
One Park Avenue, New York, N.Y. 10016.
Printed in the United States of America
Library of Congress Catalog Card Number: 72–80840
ISBN: 0-517-500582
Fifth Printing, July, 1977

ACKNOWLEDGMENTS

We are grateful to Mr. Frank Turek of Laguna Hills, California, who built Frank's Picture Framing to success and sold the business to us upon his retirement. We hasten to thank Calvin Pedranti, an artist now in residence in San Francisco, whom we "inherited" as our first finisher, and who "taught us how to measure." To our knowledge, Cal invented the gold leaf fillet.

Ben Johnson, Jr., our great friend and erstwhile cut-and-join man, obligingly posed for pictures. Photographs taken in the finishing room involve Howard Newcomb, our finisher at that time.

CONTENTS

INTRODUCTION

THE picture framer's skills are many and varied. He has the delicate hand of a surgeon and the stamina of a bricklayer; the imagination and know-how of an engineer, and the impeccable taste of a seasoned connoisseur. He is as indispensable as a plumber and as anonymous as a stagehand; as trusted as a pediatrician and as self-taught as Abraham Lincoln. He is part interior decorator, part mechanic, part salesman, and part bookkeeper. He is master, in fact, of more skills than most people acquire in a lifetime, yet there are no schools where his trade can be learned, and fewer than a dozen books have been published about his profession. He has learned the business through apprenticeship, a love affair with his golden hands, trial, error, invention, discovery, and—it is true—filching ideas from other framers. He operates within a framework of paradoxes.

First of all, there are simply no schools that teach the art of picture framing. Some trade schools might teach something about making a frame, and even a bit of finishing such as distressing or antiquing, but building a picture frame is a minuscule and fairly unimportant facet of the whole business. And while art students occasionally learn to cut a mat of some sort, it is taught as a secondary skill, as a money-saving device for presentation of art work, and can hardly be considered a step toward learning a profession. Craft shops here and there give instruction in laying gold leaf, and certain wood-carvers even teach their trade, but most of this instruction is directed toward the dedicated hobbyist, and is seldom offered with professional picture framing in mind. The chances are strong indeed that an artist, an architect, a decorator, a designer, even a potential picture framer, can go through junior high and high school, trade school and art school, college and graduate school without ever being exposed to as little as a lecture on picture framing.

Secondly, it is surprising but unfortunately true that few books are available on the subject. And this at a time of explosive creativity across the country when husbands and wives are doing their own decorating and more and more Americans are painting, collaging, and stitching, to say nothing of collecting and displaying family heirlooms, precious photographs, and other memorabilia. What few books one can find usually concentrate on building and finishing a frame, with perhaps a few instructions for measuring, cutting, and covering mats and liners. The area of preliminary design—the master plan, so to speak—is omitted from most books on picture framing. Since this is the basis of all serious picture framing, as well as the major point of disagreement among professional framers, the public is entitled to a brisk discussion of this all-important phase of the business.

Third, the framer works in almost total anonymity. His profession is surrounded by an aura of non-recognition which almost suggests that a picture frames itself—referred to in the trade as "the magic-wand theory of framing." Magazine articles illustrated with pictures of beautifully decorated houses give credit to the decorator, the architect, the landscaper, the pool builder, the designers of the wallpaper, carpeting, fabrics, and table settings, and even, occasionally, to the artists whose pictures are hung on the walls; but the picture framer, in spite of the imaginative and beneficial contribution he has made to creating the surroundings, is left off the list of contributors, and is considered as worthy of mention as the carpet layer or the electrician.

Admittedly the framer shares his anonymity with other artists: the photographer whose work helps sell advertising in the national magazines but whose name is not mentioned; the commercial artist whose billboard poster is not signed; the designers of packaging, gift wrappings, and greeting cards; the writers and illustrators of brochures which arrive with utility bills and requests from charities; the window dressers and display managers whose creative know-how helps sell a department store's products. These artists are usually recognized at an annual banquet, when awards are handed out for "Best of Everything"; the picture framer earns his reward when he pastes his label to the back of a framed picture and sends it out of the shop to be enjoyed.

This is not a how-to book for the simple reason that professional picture framing is not a how-to project. Material is here for do-it-yourselfers who might want to ferret it out, but we are discussing the art of picture framing from the professional's point of view, and we hope to dispel at once the popular notion that a framing shop is a cross between Santa's workshop and the fairytale shoemaker's basement, operated nocturnally by elves.

Another popular misconception of picture framing is that a framer makes his living by framing the work of art students and Sunday painters. Art students are notoriously poor in pocket, and painters are, understandably, bargain hunters. If the framer had no other customers than these, he would quickly starve to death or have to hang up a sign (and we actually saw one): "Also, umbrellas mended, cornet lessons, keys made, anything wired for a lamp."

Actually, the picture framer's list of customers is five miles long and as diversified as the Yellow Pages: public utilities, insurance companies, banks, hospitals, and unions—to mention a few. The rent is paid by advertising agencies, architects, medical groups, airlines, and on and on.

Large corporations cannot seem to operate—and ours certainly would not—without photographs of politicians and celebrities, presidents of clubs and societies, ground-breakings and ribbon-cuttings, and group pictures of gatherings of far-flung corporation officials. Then there are business licenses, certificate awards, office jokes, diplomas, citations and bulletins, ad proofs for agencies, and prospectus covers for brokerage offices—the bread and butter of the framing profession.

Opportunities for more imaginative framing are possible when lobbies and offices are decorated with framed pictures. Architects want their prospective clients to see architectural renderings framed on the walls. Oil companies and development advisers display their real estate holdings and operating methods. Thus picture framing, while seemingly a small part of commerce, probably touches as many segments of business as any other field we can think of, including banks and utility companies.

Even much of the original artwork that comes through the shop is commercial in origin. "Commercial" artists are so called because much of their work is used to sell a product, and does not imply that they are not artists in the truest sense of the word: many commercial artists have a better sense of color, design, and execution than those artists whose framed pictures are sold through department stores, furniture showrooms, and art galleries. Many commercial artists teach on the side and do serious painting.

Farther along we mention framing for "on-going shows," and *Westways* magazine is a good case in point : * we frame original artwork that constitutes its cover art as well as many illustrations that appear throughout the magazine. (The original art director of *Westways* is said to have given a professional boost to more artists and illustrators in Southern California than any other single person, insisting on using original art in every issue, and that by local artists.) Our local Society of Illustrators, which ties in closely with similar groups in San Francisco and New York, has at least one group show going on at all times, and competition is heavy for national recognition. The shows are expanded from year to year, and we are challenged to create new and unusual framing. Calling it commercial doesn't preclude the art aspect.

Framers operate in as many ways, perhaps, as there are framers, and have probably gone into business for as many reasons. We bought an established business some years ago and promptly fell in love with it. Within a year we realized how little most people know about it, how fascinating it really is, and how helpful we might be if we divulged some of the ideas we have developed and some of the tricks we have stumbled onto that might be of help not only to other framers but also to decorators, professional and amateur, and the public in general. We don't claim to know all there is to know, and we haven't even made our first million, but it is a business that we know and love, and we want others to understand why.

* The official publication of the Automobile Club of Southern California, and the second oldest continuously published magazine in the United States.

Sponge rubber pads on the bottom corners of the frame prevent tipping after the picture is hung, and also prevent dust from settling along the wall behind the frame.

The Picture Framer's Handbook

1 THE "OTHER ARTIST"

THE expression "custom framing," which most professional framers do not particularly like, is still the best appellation for an individually designed, hand-crafted framing job. Custom framing provides the customer with many advantages that simply do not exist in the area of ready-made frames. Primarily and obviously, he has access to the framer's design experience; also, he has a wider choice of mat boards and fabrics, and he can pinpoint his selection of a finish to the slightest difference between one color and another, the degree of goldness, and the amount of antiquing. A crafted frame is cut and joined by hand to the desired measurement, glued and nailed at the corners, and hand-finished as a unit, with mitred corners sealed. The mat is cut by hand, and the liner is covered in one piece of fabric, showing no ragged mitres. It is, after all, the same old story of service—one simply gets a better and more durable job at the hands of a professional, whether he be

3

a carpet layer, an upholsterer, a plumber, a drapery maker, or a house painter.

It is possible to get ready-made frames of fine quality, carefully built and finished, and many of the good moulding companies carry them; however, one is limited to stock sizes. Ready-made frames that are priced to sell inexpensively are knocked out by machine and often held together at the corners by only one nail or even by right-angle staples, which tend to allow the frame to fall apart or at least to separate at the corners, after only a little handling. When such frames are designed for oil paintings, they usually consist of a 1-inch liner cut from precovered white linen liner, which, when joined, shows a distracting mitre; and a 3-, 4-, or even 5-inch frame souped up with gesso and lacquer and spotted with spray gold, appropriate—even if the liner were in proper proportion—to one painting out of twenty.

On the other hand, frames such as one finds in variety stores and drugstores and even at the local supermarket have proved to be a real boon to amateur photographers, sketchpad artists, doting parents, and organizations purchasing in quantity. An advertising agency for instance may hand out token awards to a hundred or more clients, or a school may decide to give framed diplomas to the entire graduating class; ready-made frames are entirely adequate for such occasions and can be had at substantially lower cost. Such frames come complete with glass, stapled fitting devices, backing, and a hanger (and perhaps even an out-dated photograph of a favorite movie star). The custom framer, however, must handle each frame individually, cut each piece of glass, fit each subject by hand, and, of course, charge accordingly.

We frequently advise a customer, in the interest of saving money or if the artwork is to be used on a temporary basis, to let us cut a fillet and mat, or custom-cover a liner, to a ready-made frame. Such a seemingly magnanimous relinquishment of professional skill only serves to point up one of our principal theories—the frame is probably the least important component of framing. From a business standpoint, such an attitude creates good will.

While we are talking about frames that compete—or, rather, that do not compete—with the professional framer, we may as well mention some others. Plaquing is a form of framing with which most of the public is familiar, and while this provides a permanent housing for diplomas and certificates, it offers little variation in design (except for color) and is usually somewhat more expensive than custom framing. While the plaquing process can seldom be reversed, plaqued subjects can be successfully framed if a decorator chooses to soften the somewhat institutionalized appearance of plaquing, or decides to bring a more elegant look to office walls.

4 Section frames are still another variation in the field of ready-made frames. These are packaged two equal sides to a unit, including hardware for joining the corners, and are available in walnut and in various treatments

on aluminum (pewter, gold, black). Available in lengths from 8 to 50 inches, these sections allow the mixing of various pairs to create a variety of sizes. An amateur artist could, for example, buy two 16s, two 20s, and two 24s, and by interchanging the sizes have three frames readily at hand. Section frames are marketed as do-it-yourself items, but some practice is required before the amateur becomes competent and confident about fitting a large section frame with glass. Considerable glass has been broken because it all sounds so easy. The custom framer is happy to sell section frames not only because they are more expensive than frames he makes to serve a similar purpose, but also because he makes a considerable fitting fee if the amateur is uncertain of his own success. Metal section frames are available in two depths, one to accommodate a drawing, mat, glass, and backing, and a deeper size to accommodate a canvas on stretcher bars. Quite aside from the convenience, metal frames contribute substantially to the current demand for slick decor.

Plastics are coming on strong in the area of ready-made frames, although the adjective must be immediately qualified, as the creator of Plexiglas frames is a skilled craftsman in his own right. To date the most successful plastic frame is a box backed by an instantly removable liner, making it possible to interchange pictures in no time at all. Such boxes can be used with mats and fillets, and supply the answer to a long-requested demand for different and contemporary framing.

Braquettes and corner frames serve two purposes: to frame temporary possessions or to fit into minuscule budgets. The former provide 3-inch strips of plastic or aluminum to be attached to the center top and bottom of a mounted picture (or a piece of glass), tightened at the back with an accompanying cord, and secured at the proper tautness by a metal clamp. This is an entirely temporary type of framing as dirt eventually seeps inside the glass and onto the subject. The same holds true for the so-called "fast frames," which consist of four small clamp-on corners and an accompanying cord, which may be adjusted to hang a picture from 4 inches to 26 inches square. These are also made in both plastic and aluminum and, like the braquettes, currently retail for two dollars a package, glass being extra.

So much for the existing threats to the professional custom framer. He may be nudged from one side or another by new inventions, changing concepts, and less expensive methods, but he'll never be moved over and out, any more than will a dependable automobile mechanic, a watchmaker, or the trusted neighborhood butcher. As long as the public has any faith at all in quality performance, good taste, and the importance of preserving beautiful possessions, there will always be a place for the "other artist."

5

$\mathcal{2}$ GLORIFYING THE TRADES

In these days of the all-American hang-up on the importance of a college degree, and the unpalatable truth that some youngsters may not be able scholastically to finish high school, we hasten to glorify the trades. We need only look around us to see that our master craftsmen are of an older generation and that most of them are not being followed by a younger. This is not due to a lack of demand for craftsmanship—certain products and services will never be supplied by machines and computers—but to an attitude toward those people who make a living by working with their hands. Our youngsters are growing up in a national atmosphere that subtly suggests they have failed if they do not go to college, if they have not made all As, or are not smart enough to become doctors, lawyers, college professors, or business executives. Hardly any red-blooded American boy says, "Daddy, I want to grow up to be a wood-carver," and even fewer parents are saying, "Son, why don't you just shoot for a C average and get into furniture making?" (Or butchering, upholstering, bricklaying, or picture framing.) The demand for wood-carvers in the picture framing trade alone is so great that prices for fine carved frames are well beyond the reach of all but the purses of the wealthy.

A skilled finisher, who should know how to read but need not have finished English Literature, can always get a good job in this unusually happy business. A good mat cutter, in his spare time, can make a decent living at home by cutting mats for artists, schools, and framers who don't cut mats. Other sources would be dealers in prints, rare books, stores that sell posters and cards, and the like. An experienced fitter can usually get a job within a day or two after landing in a new town or after leaving another job.

A knowledge of mathematics is mandatory in the framing business, but "golden hands" are even more important. (Such hands inevitably can learn a wide variety of other skills.) The youngster who has been urged to lay aside his model cars and planes in favor of getting grades for college may have been robbed of enjoying his life's work, and a thoughtful parent is wise to encourage the development of manual dexterity along with mental gymnastics. It may come as quite a shock to the education-oriented parent to discover that his child is an artist instead of a scholar; it may also come as a shock for the parent to learn that an artist doesn't necessarily have to be described as "starving." The entire field of crafts and trades is wide open to anyone who cares to master one or many of them.

We must face the fact that most college students are there because it is the thing to do and because of a greater earning potential than their high-school-graduate cousins. But times are changing and there is a renewed interest in the trades.

More and more we see and read about adult drop-outs who have come to the sudden realization that a lucrative desk job is not as rewarding as, for instance, turning clay on a potter's wheel. The hard-hitting salesman, while maintaining a split-level home, two cars, and an expensive wife, wakes up one morning and finds that he is more at peace with himself and the world around him when he is working in leather or creating jewelry. Suddenly the possibility exists of a life richer, more creative, and probably more rewarding spiritually. Too many of us are poured into the stream of business life, not even considering along the way that there might conceivably be a choice in the matter of life style.

Surely it is now time for parents and educators to realize that American skills are as important as American brains, and to reevaluate the purposes of education. Every parent dreams of a life of fulfillment for his child. Why should that fulfillment be presumed to come only from having mastered a given number of academic courses in a given number of schools?

It would be a great day indeed if the American dream could embrace this basic fact of life: there isn't much sense in learning to make a good living if one is to go through life not honestly loving what one is doing. Happy is the one who can honestly say, "I may get tired, but I don't get tired of what I'm doing."

3 DESIGN

GOOD framing starts with good design, and this is where the competition begins. The customer who recognizes that his picture looks better framed than it did unframed has found himself a picture framer, and he will usually change framers about as quickly as he changes dentists. It behooves the framer, obviously, to acquire as many loyal, faithful, talkative customers as he can get, and it all begins when he brings total attention, studied imagination, and genuine interest to what the customer is having framed. Nothing alienates a customer as quickly as to be asked, "What do you have in mind for a frame?" An overwhelming majority of the public has little or no knowledge of what framing is all about, so the customer expects and deserves professional assistance.

No single rule of thumb can be applied to what constitutes good framing, but our basic adage is this: a picture framed correctly and tastefully may be used in any room, in any home, in any office. This is not to say that there is only one way to frame a given picture—in some instances a dozen variations in design could do it ample justice—and, in fact, much of the time a better job of design is achieved if we know where the picture is to hang and how the customer intends to use it. The same watercolor print, for instance, is appropriate in a bedroom, an entrance hall, a streamlined office, or a bathroom. A suitable fillet, a neutral mat, a simple walnut frame and glass constitute adequate framing; however, gold may be introduced into the design if the picture is to hang in a bedroom. Eye-catching color is good thinking for an entrance hall; the sharp, clean lines of a gold-topped walnut frame, or even an aluminum section frame, blend with the decor of a modern office; and a somewhat elaborate, decorative frame suggests itself for a bathroom.

Corner samples of frames, liners, mats, and fillets are the tools of the designer's trade. He develops and demonstrates his ideas by means of these visual aids, and while the customer may have difficulty understanding how the finished product is going to look ("I can't visualize it." "Don't worry— most people can't.") he just has to take the framer's word for it. Many of our customers say they come to us because they have fun getting involved in plans for a picture. While a designer can't fake an attitude of enthusiasm, he can surely show enough genuine interest to gain the customer's confidence.

Design is a positive art, but we almost have to approach it from a negative position. Careful consideration and considerable observation have led us to the conclusion that major mistakes in designing stem from these points:

> Mats or liners or both too wide or too narrow (the latter is the more frequent mistake and the worse of the two, as the picture appears cramped into the frame).
> Misuse of colors and fabrics.
> Inappropriate frames.
> Lack of proportion between mat and frame, or liner and frame.

Esthetically, mats and liners serve the same purpose, differing only in that they are used on different types of subjects for different functional reasons; thus a mat or liner is used as a visual separation between picture and frame, so that the eye relates directly to the picture, not really seeing the frame but accepting the framed picture as a complete unit, a satisfying whole. When the mat or liner is too narrow to create a visual separation, the frame seems to close in on the picture, defeating all the purposes of framing. Using a 1-inch linen liner on a large oil painting, and surrounding it by a 3- or 4-inch fancy frame with gesso and spotted color and spotted gold is shockingly poor design, regardless of its all too frequent occurrence. If the proportions were reversed—a 4-inch liner and a 1-inch frame—the painting would have a better chance to speak for itself, which is what framing is all about, after all.

10

Corner samples are the tools of the designer's trade.

While too narrow a separation is the more frequent error, too wide a separation sometimes occurs, with somewhat less disastrous results. If the mat or liner is too wide, the picture seem to huddle in an oversized space. Inasmuch as 6- or 7-inch mats are sometimes used by a decorator as a space-filling gimmick, we probably should not let it affect our blood pressure; the subject was selected as a decorative item in the first place and probably will not be looked at much anyway.

MATS

As a general rule, good mat proportion consists of $2\frac{1}{2}$ inches at the top and sides and 3 inches at the bottom. Larger pictures can handle 3- and $3\frac{1}{2}$-inch mats, and even as wide as $4\frac{1}{2}$ and 5 inches. Anything wider than the last stops being functional and becomes decorative. Smaller pictures use smaller mats, although we are inclined to frown on anything narrower than $1\frac{1}{2}$ and 2 inches. (A colored mat can be somewhat narrower than a neutral one since color presents an immediate impact and can be stopped more suddenly by the frame.) If the customer insists on too narrow a mat, we switch from mat to liner; a 1-inch liner creates a more logical effect than a 1-inch mat.

LINERS

Technically the word liner can be used interchangeably with the word insert, although the term insert may be somewhat misleading as it is not an inserted frame at all but rather is the first liner of the frame's design and is cut to the size of the picture. The first liner is usually $\frac{3}{8}$- to $\frac{1}{2}$-inch wide and is gold, silver, or sprayed with colored lacquer. Occasionally the first liner can go as wide as $\frac{3}{4}$ inch if it is to be covered in a colored linen and topped by a wider, neutral linen liner. A wider liner is also used when covered with velvet—less velvet would not be enough and more would be too much. Most paintings stand up well to a 2- or $2\frac{1}{2}$-inch linen-covered liner. One-inch liners should be used only on small paintings, and then only with a narrower frame. Too often a 1-inch liner covered in white linen or black velvet is used with a 3-inch carved or compo frame; the overall effect is one of utter suffocation.

COLORS AND FABRICS

It may seem arrogant for us to express our opinion in an area that seems to involve only personal taste, yet we have not only strong opinions but some valid reasons for them. For instance, there is an all-too-prevalent tendency to think in terms of black and white—white mat, black frame. Black and white are the strongest colors we have and should be used sparingly, and then only if a touch of boldness is required. Mat board comes in so many gradations of white that it is possible to achieve the look of white while

A Cézanne lithograph print (mounted and trimmed) is measured for ⅜-inch gold liner, plus 2½-inch liner covered with linen, plus slant-back stem.

softening the overall effect. As for a black frame, a walnut frame with a teak or black walnut finish gives the effect of black, but the starkness of black is toned down by the grain of the wood. Even white linen is less glaring than white mat board, and lends a richness that tends to subdue the startling effect of white. Certificates normally framed in black lacquer frames take on a more important look if gold is used, to tie in with a seal, or colored lacquer to pick up a detail from a logo. In short, an imaginative designer usually begins by resisting a black frame; about the only picture that can stand up to a white mat and black frame is a black and white one.

Color is also frequently misused to fill a decorating scheme: "The room needs green, so I need green mats." Green is properly brought into the room by means of greens in a picture, but a green mat will serve only to stifle it. To bring out the greens in a picture, we would suggest a green fillet, a well-chosen neutral mat, and a green lacquer frame. The picture is always boss, and it is nothing short of a dirty trick to ask it to be anything but what it is, an enhancement to the wall. If more green is needed in a room, a mirror could be framed with a green velvet or linen liner and a greener frame; thus the decorating problem is solved and a picture is saved to be used at another time, on another wall, in another room.

When selecting a color for a mat, fillet, or lacquered liner, we usually work with the least important color in the picture; by relating the eye to the smallest color area, the larger areas of color—those which the artist intended as the main part of the picture—become more pronounced and, regardless of what is done with a mat or linen liner and frame, the look of the finished product is total.

Mat board comes in a wide variety of colors, some bold, some subtle. Usually we reserve the bold-colored mat board to fillets, but occasionally a cartoon or a bit of whimsy suggests a colored mat, and this in no way contradicts what we have just said about bringing color into a room by way of a mat. Some subjects are improved by the use of a bold-colored mat; others are offended by it. A wall sparked by color is certainly more interesting than one held down to drab, neutral colors, and that is why we like to design with colored lacquer frames from time to time. A wall full of certificates framed in ½-inch black frames can be quite dull (if informative), but if the frames pick up a detail of color—even if only by matching a signature in blue ink—the wall becomes more interesting. Sometimes it is wise to match the color of the frame to the color of the fillet; sometimes we repeat the color of the mat in the color of the frame, adding enough black to darken the color so the frame is a definitive containment. Subtly colored mat boards (pewter, sauterne, olive) work absolute wonders on architectural renderings which, after all, are original art and deserve selective treatment. It is sometimes difficult to guide a conservative customer away from conventional (white) mats for functional office framing, but when we do the tasteful effect is so startling and interesting that he usually stays converted.

Contrary to a much-accepted notion that the framer's favorite fabric is burlap, he uses a wide selection of linens, silks, satins, and velvets, and burlap as little as possible. Burlap is so porous as to be difficult to work with, as glue must be applied with extreme care or it seeps through the fabric. Loosely woven as it is, the warp and woof cannot be lined up at good, sharp right angles, so the end result looks clumsy and unprofessional. Textured linens, available in a wide variety of colors, are easier to work with and create a smarter, more finished appearance. Heavy textures should be used carefully, and are best as backgrounds for shadow boxes, liners on rugged seascapes, ceramics, and wooden or metal panels.

Fine-textured linens are desirable on photographs, watercolors, pastels, prints, and renderings, or on any subject that calls for neutral or delicate treatment. Fabrics whose warp and woof are of contrasting colors and textures (rough-looking fabrics interweaving brown and white, for instance) are totally unworkable as they set up a busyness with which no picture can compete. The rare exception might be a fine-textured Oriental silk whose warp and woof blend with colors in a Chinese embroidery. Silks and satins should be selected with loving care and with a regard for sheen; shiny fabrics set up a reaction that usually constitutes a distraction instead of an enhancement.

Velvet is the most elegant fabric we work with, but again it should be used sparingly and discriminately. We feel that velvet is inappropriate to the delicacy of watercolors, the subject matter of seascapes, and the nature of pastels. One decorator "tie-in" that we deplore is matting with velvet to match velvet throw pillows regardless of the subject matter of the pictures. If a repetition of velvet is the reason for the decoration, a mirror can be used (as we mentioned before in connection with color) or a shadow box containing a plate or family heirlooms.

Velvet is sometimes used to cover a mat for a portrait photograph or some other subject that should be covered by glass. In this instance it is well to put the glass directly on the subject, leaving the velvet mat exposed. When a picture with a velvet mat is glazed, the velvet tends to crush flat at the four corners, distracting from its richness. Little harm can come to the exposed velvet if it is brushed occasionally with a clean paintbrush, and if visitors are cautioned not to touch it—which they invariably do anyway.

The customer saves little money by providing his own fabric. Not all fabrics adapt to use by the framer, as many are too fine to accept white glue (ginghams, chambrays, and many silks), others are too coarse to "turn" onto mats and liners, and others fray too readily to be workable. Velveteen cannot be used as a substitute for velvet as it separates when it is turned, exposing the background and destroying the purpose behind the elegance of velvet. The framer knows what fabrics he can work with successfully and the little

Some of the fabrics we use: Oriental silk; beige linen; heavier-textured linen; velvet.

money the customer hopes to save by providing his own fabric is often eaten up in labor costs incurred in handling unfamiliar materials.

FRAMES

Much inappropriate framing stems from the impact of gallery framing— the goldness of the Louvre, the elaborately carved frames in Italy and Spain. It is almost as if the public believes that if it's carved, gold, elaborate, and expensive, it must be good. So much prestige has been given to the carved or compo frame that, unfortunately, it is often considered appropriate to any painting at all. Art dealers and galleries usually keep on hand frames of this type, fitting new paintings to their "warehouse" frames, regardless of how the frame makes or breaks the picture. The picture buying public assumes that dealers and galleries are authorities on framing and accepts their inappropriate standards of framing without question. We consider gold, compo or carved, wide frames illogical on pastels, photographs, watercolors, graphics, and oil paintings whose subjects do not relate to elaborate frames, such as seascapes. The subject of the painting is as important a consideration in design as are the colors and the medium.

The term "antique gold and white" has crept into the public's consciousness probably via furniture and department stores, and is considered elegance personified and the epitome of good framing by many misinformed. "Don't you think it brings out the white in the picture?" Rarely is antique gold and white a desirable finish, and it certainly does not "bring out the white" in a picture. As we have said before, white is seldom an appropriate color to use in framing, and it actually kills whites in a picture. This can be proved dramatically by placing a white corner sample on one corner of a picture and a walnut or dark green corner on the other. The white areas of the picture leap to one's attention when contrasted to the dark-toned frame.

While overframing probably occurs with greater frequency, underframing can be just as distressing and disastrous. It grieves us to see a decorator insist on a 1/2-inch black half-round (the standard, old-fashioned certificate frame) for a hand-colored engraving, especially when he has also ordered a gold leaf fillet and a linen-covered mat. A 3/4-inch walnut moulding with no liner is an illogical and inadequate frame for an old world oil painting, and we would hardly use a shiny gold frame for an old family photograph or an icon on distressed wood.

PROPORTIONS BETWEEN MAT, LINER, AND FRAME

Proper proportion between mat and frame or liner and frame is another of the designer's considerations. The liner and frame should not be of equal widths, nor should the liner be the same width as any part of the frame, such as a panel or a compo detail. Again there is a reason: repetition of the same width is not only monotonous, but it stops the eye twice at the same point,

17

causing a reaction to the frame rather than to the picture. This mistake is not as easily made when a mat is used, as few pictures requiring a mat are framed in a moulding as wide as a mat.

We frequently encounter a customer with an aversion to linen liners, or whose wall space is so small as to preclude use of a liner. Insisting as we do that there be some visual separation between picture and frame, we use a $\frac{3}{8}$- or $\frac{1}{2}$-inch liner in gold or silver or colored lacquer inside the frame; this separation can also be effected by using a moulding that combines gold and color, the details of the moulding becoming part of the design. This is especially true if the frame "reads" from the picture out: $\frac{1}{4}$-inch gold, $\frac{3}{4}$-inch colored lacquer that picks up a color from the picture, $\frac{1}{2}$-inch gold at the edge of the frame. Separation and proportion are thus taken care of without the use of extra liners.

More than two liners inside a frame is a contrivance that serves no purpose but to put extra money into the framer's pocket (especially if three velvet liners are used, as has been done). A double fillet under a mat, however, creates a superbly subtle effect when high styling is required, as on a prestigious photograph, an important etching or serigraph, or a piece that is frankly decorative. A Gregorian chant on parchment provides a good example. These pieces are usually printed in black with some illumination in gold and in red. A red fillet can be topped by a gold leaf fillet, and both topped by a mat of the parchment background color. The double fillet serves

These 8- by 10-inch prints will be matted by avocado mat board with three openings. Three choices for the frame in foreground—darker green lacquer, gold, or walnut.

A Mexican bark painting will be attached on top of colored linen and framed with a ¾-inch walnut, borghese shape frame. It would be a shame to cover the irregular edges of the bark painting, as they represent much of the charm of the piece.

to act almost as a repetition of the illumination. The frame can then be gold or black or red, as it is really not much more important than the binding on the book from which the chant was removed. The double fillet is usually more effective if one is done in gold or silver leaf, but two colors may be used to play against each other, under a neutral or fabric mat.

In many cases, as with Mexican bark paintings or an original graphic or a child's treasured drawing, the edge of the paper plays an important part, such as the rough edges on the bark paintings, a lovely deckle edge torn against wickedly expensive paper, or the torn edge of the sack the child drew on. In these cases (and others) the framing is designed to show the edges. Bark paintings, which are seldom glazed, can be attached on top of a wild-colored mat board or even colored or neutral linen. The child's drawing could be handled in the same way—and glazed, since it probably doesn't make that much difference whether glass comes in contact with the subject. A good graphic, however, must be separated from glass. In this instance it is well to select a colored mat board, picking up a color from the print, affix the print to the mat board, then cut a wider mat to indicate that the intention is to show the deckle edge.

While it is readily understandable that decorators, architects, industrial designers, and others in the creative field are always striving for new ap-

19

proaches and different effects, such inventiveness can be a framer's headache. Further, it often increases costs beyond reason. A consultation with a knowledgeable framer, before plans are drawn, can save many hours at the drawing board for a job that could have been done more easily and at less expense. An instance of this situation might be: a designer decides to use a $\frac{1}{4}$-inch moulding 2 inches deep, and all his specifications have been drawn up with the expectation that such a moulding is available. Since it is not, the framer has to rip the top from a wider moulding, sand the raw edge, invent some way of holding the picture in with such a narrow rabbet and fragile frame and, of course, charge five or six times more than he might, had he done the job with conventional moulding. Another instance might be the addition of, say, antiquing to a stock-finished frame; two years later the decorator who ordered it (or the client) wants to duplicate the frame, often in another city or another shop. By the time the finisher has figured out how the additional treatment was done, and does it, labor costs have increased three- or fourfold, and the finished picture doesn't really look that much better.

The framer's favorite customers are those beautiful people who bring or send their pictures and say "Surprise me." In such a situation the designer can go all out with double fillets, colored linen liners, leafed inserts, and other imaginative gimmicks. On-going jobs, such as framing for decorators' showrooms or a continuing collection of illustrations, tax the ingenuity of the designer and framer, but also provide him with much pleasure. It is

A fillet with compo bead will be topped by a red fillet, topped by a white mat, and framed with a half-inch frame in red lacquer.

always a challenge to try to top himself, but the reward he reaps from ooh's and aah's and loud huzzahs is worth every minute of brain-picking.

It is not for the framer to say what is art and what is not, and it isn't really fair for a customer to ask him. "The first oil painting I ever did" might be a complete fiasco of color and design, but the framer must learn to treat each picture with the loving care that the owner rightfully feels it deserves. Actually, when a picture is woefully bad, the designer can frequently—in fact usually—make it look almost good by proper designing. We have already indicated in no uncertain terms that the reverse is also true.

The mention of an oil painting reminds us that we should like to dispel a popular notion that an original oil painting is the epitome of fine art. An artist may make a name for himself by painting *Seascape at Sunrise* one week and *Seascape at Sunset* the next, and the public is conned into the belief that the possession of one of these paintings is the equivalent of owning

Components of framing an ivory miniature. Left to right: background mount; mat in which ivory was countersunk; gold leaf fillet; paper-covered mat; frame.

Overframing as a bit of whimsy on a Persian ivory painting. The mat and frame are covered with art papers.

a Rembrandt. Just as original are etchings, engravings, silk-screen prints, batiks, intaglios, and watercolors. We haven't gone into a discussion of these art processes because so many good books are available, written by the artists who do the work and by the printers who print them. We are only the "other" artists.

PRICES

Since pricing is usually done at the design table, this is probably the time to discuss it. Depending on what town and part of town the shop is in, the reputation of the framer and his opinion of his work, to say nothing of his scruples, the cost of framing the same picture can, and does, vary from as little as 15 dollars to as much as 75 dollars. We are as appalled at the framer who deigns to charge 15 dollars as we are at the gall and audacity of charging 75 dollars. Quality of workmanship and imaginative design vary as much from one shop to another as price and, sadly, there often isn't much relationship between the two. It is distressing but true that bad design and poor workmanship frequently demand and fetch unreasonable prices, and the inexperienced customer can really be had by an unscrupulous framer, who, in all fairness, just might be trying to make some money in a business for which he is unsuited.

Regardless of design, quality, location, and reputation, pricing is still a most difficult aspect of the business and cannot be standardized. Basically price is determined by size: amount of moulding, size of mat, size of glass, size of mounting board; but then the extras start creeping in, such as difficulty of mounting, unusual fitting problems, finishing, time limit. The framer measures the frame, figures it at X dollars a foot, adds his costs for material and labor, and then includes rent and utilities, taxes, stationery and postage, backing and wrapping paper, tape, screw eyes and wire—all two-for-a-penny items that nonetheless add up—and comes up with a figure that is fair but realistic. Thus the customer has to pay the price asked for any given job, bearing in mind that he should expect his money's worth, as he does in any other area where he is paying for quality.

The moulding and supply companies are most helpful in suggesting prices and even offer charts for distribution within the trade, suggesting a trend toward standardization. It is immediately obvious, however, that there is no way to standardize, say, a fitting charge on a 16- by 20-inch subject, which might be a pencil sketch in a frame with glass, or a shadow box involving velvet and a dozen medals. It is even difficult to quote a standard price on glass: a small shop owner, operating on a tight budget and in small quarters, might have to order one light of 30- by 40-inch glass to complete a job, forcing him to pass the extra expense of ordering in small quantity on to his customer, whereas a larger, more affluent shop has space to store entire boxes of glass, purchased in quantity at wholesale prices, a saving that it can, if so inclined, pass on to the customers. The same formula holds true with regard to mat board, moulding, and mounting board: the framer's expenses vary so within the framework of his particular operation that price standardization is virtually out of the question. If one is shopping for price, one can usually find a framer who will fit into one's budget.

While we are wont to say—and stick with it—that we have a no-discount policy, personalities sometimes enter into pricing. The customer who pays promptly is given a better price break than the one on whom we have to spend extra time and bookkeeping hours to get our money; the customer who eats up two and three hours' time at the design table surely has to pay more than the one who takes only a few minutes for a decision. Then there is that special breed—all businesses have them and learn to spot them—for whom we can't do anything right. These are the poor unfortunates (usually women, but woe betide if they are male!) who apparently get out of bed in the morning with plans for making life wretched for everyone they encounter. "I thought it would be a little more gold." "This isn't the moulding I ordered." "Why is the mat crooked?" The framer learns to spot this type and add extra

23

fitting charges in case the job must be done over. Chances are strong, however, that he can tell the chronic complainer, "Leave it and we'll fix it," and put it on the pickup shelf, secure in the assumption that the second time around the objections will be forgotten and the "flaws" acceptable.

Extra fitting charges are made when a picture is put into a used frame. This may surprise the customer who thought that he could get a new print put into an old frame for a dollar or two. Glass has to be cleaned—a grimier job than cleaning new glass—and old, dried glue must be scraped away. The frame almost always has to be touched up a bit, where dust and grease have taken a toll. In short, re-fitting to an old frame is more time-consuming and more trouble than fitting to a new frame.

Many framers are expected to, and do, give discounts to interior decorators, architects, photographers, department stores, and artists. We don't go along with this notion, believing as we do that we should expect to be paid for quality regardless of the customer, and that it is the business of the individual or company asking for a discount to price the job accordingly. We fail to see why we should price a forty-dollar job at twenty to give a decorator or department store the equivalent of a *pourboire*. This is one standardization we should like to see happen in the framing business: the custom framer standing pat on straight retail prices, leaving wholesaling to shops geared to handle that type of business.

Another step forward (for standardization) would be an understanding among all framers and the public that no job can be done for under five dollars, just as it costs that much or more to turn the knob of a doctor's or dentist's front door.

One other major factor in pricing is one that we still have not been able to establish: what should we charge for knowing how to do it? Where else could this customer have gone to get a job like this, particularly if there is a time limit on it, regardless of what he might have to pay? A 10-opening mat involving circles, ovals, squares, and rectangles, covered in velvet and produced within a week, is not a run-of-the-mill job that just any frame shop can turn out. Do we charge twenty dollars more for that skill? Fifty? Two hundred?

All professional framers have to ask this question, and we probably will never get an answer until the public understands more fully how many skills the framer must have and what problems are involved in his craftsmanship.

4 MATS

THE primary and utilitarian purpose of a mat is to provide a separation between the subject and the glass that protects it from deteriorating influences such as smoke, grease, light, heat, and soot, once it is hung on the wall. But because it is such a wondrous and flexible component of framing, it serves any number of other purposes. Beyond its use as a buffer, its next, and just as important, purpose is to surround the picture with a proper and tasteful visual separation from the frame so that a look of totality is achieved. More subtly, a mat can play tricks on the eye that improve the overall impact, creating illusions that are more pleasurable than if the mat weren't there.

The first illusion has to do with a peculiarity of the human eye: if asked to locate the center of a horizontal line, the eye does a remarkably accurate job of finding the number of inches from the outside points to the center of the line. If on the other hand it is asked to locate the center of a vertical line, it will invariably spot the center as much as an inch above true center. To compensate for this universal idiosyncrasy, a properly cut mat should be at least $\frac{1}{2}$ inch wider at the bottom than it is on the top and sides, making the picture *seem* to be in the center of the frame. If a mat is cut to the same dimensions all the way around, the picture, because of the way the eye sees, seems to be falling forward out of the frame. Interestingly enough, the viewer realizes that something is wrong with his reaction to the picture, but he doesn't know what it is. In any number of instances we are able to cut a new mat to proper proportions, and the picture is saved. Dramatic improvements may be effected by means of a new mat. If the customer has a framed picture that has "something wrong with it but I don't know what it is," it is usually because the mat is too white, too narrow, and cut to the same dimensions all around. Substituting colored mat board for white compensates for the narrowness of a mat (colored mat board doesn't constrict a picture as much as stark white), and by cropping the subject only $\frac{1}{4}$ inch top and bottom, the extra $\frac{1}{2}$ inch may be picked up on the bottom of the mat. Thus the existing frame and glass are retained, and the new customer saves money to be spent the next time.

One notable exception to this rule about proportion is found in mats for Oriental subjects. Many Oriental originals or prints are or have been part of a scroll, on which there is frequently more space at the top and bottom than there is on the sides. To emphasize authenticity, the mat may be cut to proportions of, say, four or five inches at top and bottom and two or three inches on the sides. If the scroll reads in a horizontal position, the wider width occurs on the sides, the narrower at top and bottom.

Another exception, unavoidable, is cutting the mat to an existing frame, sometimes a headache to the conscientious mat cutter if he has to adjust proportions entirely alien to his judgment. If the mat is just too illogical, he simply leaves his label off the back of the picture; in fact, he doesn't use a label on any finished product that gives him adverse publicity since, as mentioned before, the quality of his work and the label on the back are the only publicity he gets.

Another problem the framer learns to live with is that old maps, reproductions of them, steel engravings, and many etchings are printed out of square. The original plate may have been perfectly in square, but paper must be damp when the print is struck, and as the paper dries, the shrinkage is unpredictable. A quick check of the diagonal measurements, from top left to lower right and vice versa, will tell the mat cutter if the subject is out of square and by how much. If the measurements are equal, the piece is in square; if they are not, he is behooved to cut the mat out of square to protect his reputation. Many old maps have a decorative border, frequently with illustrations or data relevant to the subject, so they should be shown. These borders state so emphatically to the human eye "I am square," that it isn't until a straight edge is laid alongside that the border shows up on an angle. Any deviation or overlap of a mat cut to straight dimensions would be classed as the mat cutter's bungle, loud and clear. He has no choice but to repeat the lie of the map, cutting the mat to conform to the out-of-square border. Thus the lie of the map is reinforced by the lie of the mat, and the eye accepts it as truth and is well pleased. (See Appendix, Out-of-square mats.)

The same type of deception must be perpetrated on most stitcheries and needlepoints, which are worked out of square by the pull of thread or yarn against the background material.

In the case of out-of-square engravings, where the mat is always cut to show the plate mark, the mat opening may be cut wider than the plate mark so that the eye loses the discrepancy through a point of space.

A fillet is produced by cutting a second mat opening of smaller dimensions than the mat, on a reverse bevel, so that only color is seen. Since mat board is manufactured by laminating colored art papers to the white background material, a line of white about $\frac{1}{16}$-inch wide shows when the bevel is cut. By cutting the fillet on a reverse bevel, a reading of white-color-white-color is avoided. The colored fillet repeats the width of the bevel on the mat, and it is hard to believe that such a tiny line can balance colors in the picture, bringing the total effect into focus. Properly used, it is a subtlety that shouts in a whisper.

A gold leaf fillet adds an unbelievable touch of elegance to watercolors, photographs, engravings, graphics, and the like. While gold is by far the most popular leaf fillet, there are times when silver, copper, borghese (silver leaf with a gold wash and delicate spatter), and even multicolored leaf can be even more effective. Gold or silver mat board or paper strips laid onto the mat are simply no substitute for a metal leaf fillet, as the whole purpose— to create a sparkling accent—is destroyed if the fillet is made from a dull material.

Mats covered entirely with metal leaf are decorative and dramatic when used correctly. An Oriental embroidery on black fabric and worked in colored and gold threads simply shouts for a repetition of gold rather than a repetition of black. With a delicate black spatter on shiny gold leaf, the mat seems to become an integral part of the embroidery itself. Christmas cards particularly lend themselves to a gold leaf mat treatment, as do icons and other religious subjects. Care must be taken to use proper proportions; if the mat is to be leafed it should be somewhat narrower than is normally chosen for a like-size mat, lest the dramatic treatment overpower the picture and spoil its effectiveness.

A step beyond the fillet is a mat with what we call inserts. This mat should be measured at least an inch wider all around than a regular mat, since the insert changes the proportion by requiring more space. Basically, a piece is cut out of the mat board anywhere from $1/2$ inch to $1\frac{1}{2}$ inches outward from the first window, spray lacquered or leafed, and set back into the mat. The effect is somewhat the same as a French mat, with a bolder look. The mat and fillet are marked on mat board; then a second set of marks is made, for example, $5/8$ inch outside the mat opening; a third set of marks is made, say, $3/8$ inch outside of that line. The twelve measurements are now cut as if each were a separate mat, and the mat is now in three pieces, one $5/8$ inch wide, one $3/8$ inch wide, and one $3\frac{1}{8}$ inches wide. It is important to mark each piece in some easily identifiable manner so that the components will be finished in the correct manner and can be easily reassembled. The fillet and the $3/8$-inch section are leafed or lacquered, then the inserts are set back in and secured with masking tape. It should be noted that from the top this deception cannot be detected. The bevels have been cut from right to left on one edge and from left to right on the other, so that the insert goes back in completely flush with the rest of the mat. This is a highly decorative mat treatment and is especially effective for framing a conversation piece. It also provides a change of pace in framing a "decorator wall" or a multiple-piece show.

Glass mats were once widely popular and seem to be making a comeback. (Even though the current trend in framing seems to be toward metal and plastic frames, the equally current trend toward nostalgia is resulting in a lot of "antique-making.") Glass mats are created by spraying two or three coats of enamel on the back of a clean piece of glass, either regular or nonglare, then scribing the mat opening and lifting out the window piece. Traditionally glass mats were black, with one or more gold lines added, somewhat in the French mat tradition. Imagination rises, and suddenly they don't have to be black, and can be quite effective with or without gold. (Dark green, light blue, or any color that comes in a spray enamel can be used, depending on the colors in the subject matter.)

A piece of glass is cut to the size of the frame, cleaned thoroughly on both sides, and sprayed to opacity with enamel and allowed to dry. Next the limits of the mat opening are marked on the coated surface with a soft pencil, which shows up even on black. The mat cutter then scribes these lines from exact corner to exact corner, with no overcuts, using a single-edged razor blade of fine quality. Then a single piece of newsprint is placed on the coated, scored surface and barely dampened, using a sponge and tap water. (Paper from a box of picture glass works as well as newsprint.) After ten or twelve minutes, the water will have opened the scored lines somewhat, allowing the framer to peel off the entire window section in a sheet that looks rather like opaque cellophane. If a gold leaf or colored line is to be added, the mat is marked and scribed again. The wet paper treatment is repeated, but left on only seven or eight minutes because the lines are closer together and will release more quickly, and the insert line pulled from the glass.

Black glass mat on black and white portrait print by Charles White.

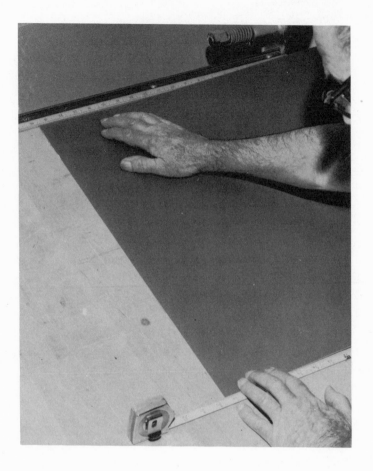

Mat board is measured on the paper cutter, the dimension double-checked at the bottom by a steel tape.

Mat board is cut to measure.

The dimensions of the mat opening are scribed to the back of the board with a compass, the sharp point of which has been filed to a rounded surface.

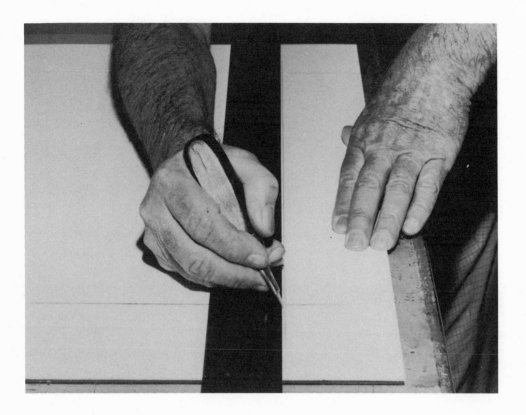

The knife begins to enter the mat board ⅛ inch above the point of intersecting mat mark-ings. The angle of the bevel is completely controlled by the steel rule and the position of the hand on the rule. (Note: The handle of the mat knife has been planed flat on one side to prevent its rolling off the table when not in use.)

Halfway down the cut, the hands are kept in the same position by the mat cutter's taking a step backward.

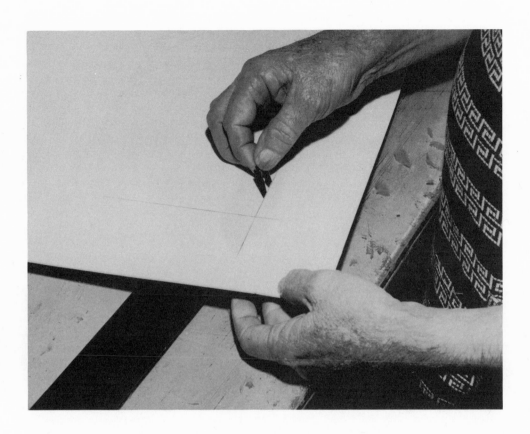

In case the cut has not been entirely clean, the window may be opened by completing the cut with a double-edged razor blade.

A fillet should be cut on a reverse bevel so that only color shows. To do this, the mat board, cut to proper outside dimensions, is placed face down and the cut mat, also face down, is laid on top and weighted. A piece of glass is held on edge and the four corners scribed inside the mat opening. The cut mat is set aside and the fillet is cut to these dimensions.

When cutting a reverse bevel (so no white shows at the window opening), the mat board is fed into the rule from the opposite direction.

Making the fourth cut on a reverse bevel.

Fillet and mat are checked out on watercolor portrait, *Mr. Robinson*, by France Borka.

The top mat is to be gold leaf fillet, hence it has been cut before the mat is cut, and marked with an X to show top. Mat material is weighted.

The fillet has been removed (note X) and the window opening of the mat is being scribed beyond the window piece of fillet. Rather than try to mark such a critical measurement with the compass, the corners are pencilled in at a distance of the thickness of a piece of glass, held upright. When all four corners have been scribed in this way, the center piece and the weight are removed, and the mat cut in the usual manner.

The technique for applying gold leaf in the insert is that used by sign painters for doing gold leaf lettering on windows or doors: a size is prepared by dissolving one gelatin capsule in a pint of warm water, then applying the size with a soft brush, a Japanese calligraphy brush being the best. The squares of 24-carat gold leaf should be scored by a fingernail into smaller pieces so that only one-third of a sheet of this expensive leaf is lifted and laid at a time. The leaf dangles in midair from the gilder's brush until it makes contact with the size, to which it is drawn as if by a magnet. The sections of leaf are overlapped like shingles or fish scales. When the circuit is complete, the leafed area is burnished gently with absorbent cotton to remove the excess leaf. One coat of leaf will not cover to opacity, so a second coat must be applied and burnished. When dry, this is stabilized with French shellac and later with a good varnish mixed with yellow pigment—the reverse order of laying leaf. Obviously this is a mat treatment that cannot be rushed or created at bargain prices.

It is well to remember that glass mats, while producing some stunning effects, do not perform the prime function of a mat—to separate the subject from the glass. If the subject matter requires separation, a fillet may be used behind the glass mat.

There are countless ways that glass mats may be varied in finish, and an entirely different effect is achieved by using non-reflecting glass, adding more possibilities for diversity. Some of the fine finishes on frames can be used for these variations, by reversing the order of application. One of our most effective finishes is achieved this way: the wood is sanded and sealed, a lacquer color applied, a delicate stipple of alcohol dyes added, and finally all are tied together with a spatter and sealed. To do this on a glass mat the process is reversed: sealer, spatter, stipple, basic color in enamel, and sealed again. A gold leaf fillet on mat board looks marvelous with this and provides the needed separation between subject and glass.

Contrary to a popular notion among fledgling artists and hopeful hobbyists, a mat is not cut with a razor blade and a yardstick as tools. Even a professional mat cutter cannot control the whip, or bend, in a razor blade as it cuts a bevel. As for cutting against a yardstick, wood is crooked and undependable, to say nothing of its being vulnerable to slicing. A good mat knife and a good steel rule are indispensable requisites for cutting mats.

Mat knives fall into two categories: one is held in the fist and the other is held between the fingers and thumb, as one holds a pencil. Each has advantages and disadvantages, but the ultimate choice as to which is more comfortable lies with the mat cutter.

The fist-held knife is probably easier for the beginner. These knives have replaceable blades that must be discarded when dull, although both ends may be used. Figuring on no more than a dozen cuts on each end of a dis-

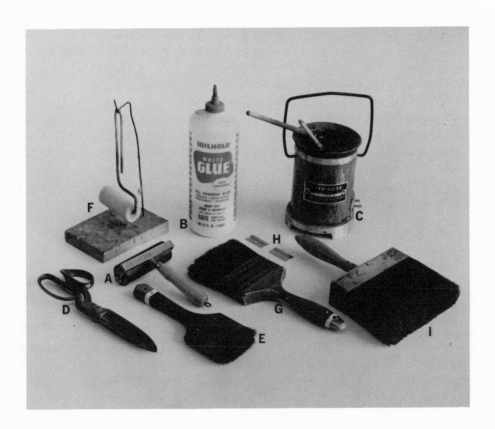

Tools for covering mats and liners:

A. Rubber brayer for laying linen and prints.

B. White glue (marketed under a variety of trade names) is used directly from the container.

C. Electric glue pot for keeping hot glue warm.

D. Efficient, dependable shears.

E. Sawed-off brush for pounding out bubbles. By sawing off the bristles a more rigid brush is obtained.

F. The sponge rubber roller is used to spread white glue. (If it is stored in a plastic bag in such a way that the roller doesn't touch the bag, and kept closed by a rubber band between uses, the roller is always immediately usable. A lot of glue is saved by not washing it down the drain after each use.)

G. Four-inch brush for laying fabric; also for brushing fabric for fitting.

H. Razor blades—used by the hundreds.

I. Seven-inch brush for laying fabric; one should be maintained for spreading wallpaper paste. This is a paperhanger's brush.

posable blade, this knife can be pretty expensive to use; it is also time-consuming, as the knife must be taken apart when the blade is adjusted or replaced. The blade may be used in three positions (that is, three different lengths may be exposed), but at its longest length it produces considerable whip—as a razor blade would—and the mat cutter may expect more curvature on a long cut than if he were using a shorter blade or a stationary one.

The second knife has a retractable blade that can be sharpened on a carborundum wheel. Slight honing may be done between sharpenings on a piece of non-glare glass or, better, on a piece of balsa wood or leather, impregnated with jewelers' rouge on one side and white diamond-cutting compound on the other, the impregnating liquid being lighter fluid. The best honing tool to date is Gerber's Sportsman's Steel, advertised as a hunter's or fisherman's knife sharpener, but indispensable to a mat cutter or a woodcarver. As the mat knife must be kept at razor sharpness at all times, investment in honing tools is advisable for the artist or hobbyist, and mandatory for the professional mat cutter.

One advantage to the retractable blade knife is that it offers a wider choice as to the length of the blade; however, neither knife can be recommended over the other, as the knife to use is the one that most comfortably fits the hand.

We find it hard to understand why so many straight-sided mats are seen, as it is easier to cut a beveled edge than a straight edge: when the knife enters the board at an angle, it opens a furrow that tends to turn the board up slightly, relieving a drag on the blade. On a straight vertical cut, the knife is fighting the grain of the board all the way. Mechanically, then, a beveled mat is more practical, besides being more eye-pleasing and versatile.

Each mat cutter must find his own most comfortable way to work, but we have developed a system that presents some practical advantages. A stationary table, waist high, has been covered with a piece of plate glass (which also serves as an extra pressing area when mounted prints stack up in the back room). Parallel to the front edge of the table we have mounted a 2- by 48-inch steel rule, fastened at each end to the glass by double-faced tape, with two 1- by 3-inch pieces of mat board separating the rule from the glass. When a mat is to be cut, the mat board is slipped under the center of the rule and the left hand holds the mat board stationary, providing a virtually immovable edge against which the knife is drawn. By arranging for the mat cutter to stand alongside his work area instead of having to reach for a long cut, he can make a 48-inch cut without having to reach beyond his arm span, by simply stepping backward as the cut is made.

44

The disadvantage to the amateur's cutting and covering his own mats is that he usually lacks the proper tools and adequate working space. However, if he is that interested, he can have lots of fun and much reward if he invests

The mat has been covered in a Chinese silk, and the window piece set into the mat opening. This will press under glass for an hour or so before turning the fabric to the back of the mat.

The covered mat is weighted for stability while the outer edges are trimmed with a single-edged razor blade.

Excess fabric has been cut from the edges and center of the covered mat and the corners mitred for turning.

Hot glue is applied and the fabric turned to the back of the mat.

A small piece of glass serves as a tool for pressing the fabric taut. (A piece of moulding will also do, and many fitters use the palm of the hand.)

Extra attention is given to the corners, here being doubly sharpened by pressing the finger-nail into the corner.

Icon of Peter and Paul (imitation). Because it was out of square, it was countersunk in temlock and built up by out-of-square fillets until the mat could be cut square. The mat has been leafed with multicolored leaf and toned down with an alcohol wash. Compo stem frame in heavy antique on lacquer.

in a few materials and tools. The first major outlay is for a *good* steel rule, a mat knife or knives, and a honing steel. He will also need

> animal glue
> white glue or Yes glue *
> a small trim roller for spreading white or Yes glue
> a good 4-inch paintbrush for laying fabric
> a 2-inch paintbrush with the bristles sawed off
> a sturdy brush for spreading hot glue
> a couple of hundred inexpensive single-edged razor blades

When a mat is to be covered with fabric, the material is cut a couple of inches larger than the outside dimensions of the mat and set aside. If white glue is used, it can be drizzled onto the mat directly from the bottle; Yes glue, diluted in a plastic jug, may be dipped out with the trim roller. It takes a while to get the feel of how much glue to use, but it is best to err on the side of over-gluing during the learning process. A temporary guide is this: fairly heavy for good sturdy linen, less for lighter fabrics, and doubly heavy for velvet and textured linens.

The glue is now rolled carefully and evenly until the entire surface of the mat is smoothly covered; more glue may be added if it rolls out too thin. There must be enough glue to make a firm bond with the fabric, but not enough to seep through. Every spot that is not covered with glue will cause a bubble in the finished mat. When the surface is right, the fabric is picked up and shaken vigorously to remove ravelings, then laid carefully over the glued mat and smoothed all over with the large paintbrush. If there are wrinkles or bubbles, these may be further smoothed by using the sawed-off brush, even using a pounding motion if the flaws are stubborn.

When the fabric has been successfully laid, the excess is trimmed from the sides by running a razor blade along the edges of the covered mat. Now the mat is turned, fabric side down, and four diagonal cuts are made from the mat corners into the mat opening, stopping one and a half inches or so from the edge of the mat opening. The excess fabric is removed from the center with a razor blade or shears.

To anchor these flaps onto the back of the mat, hot glue is applied to about an inch of the edge, and the fabric turned back, using a piece of glass (the best), the side of the hand, a piece of mat board, or a piece of wide liner, and being careful that the fabric is tight and that the bevel shows no bubbles.

---

* *Our attention has recently been called to a special mounting paste with the same properties, which produces even more satisfactory results. Called Record Brand, it is obtainable from S & W Framing Supplies, Inc., 431 Willis Avenue. Williston Park, New York, N.Y. 11596. We obtain ours locally at C. R. Laurence Co., Inc., which has offices in Los Angeles, San Jose, Dallas, and Chicago.*

(Velvet is tricky to turn because of its deep nap; care should be taken not to pull it so tight that the nap opens up, but tight enough to make sure that no excess fabric fails to attach to the mat.) The corners are especially critical as it is easy to leave them loose. If ravelings show in the corners, they may be tipped by a tiny amount of white glue on a toothpick and pressed down with pressure from the toothpick or a fingernail.

To cover a wooden liner the same steps are traced: white glue rolled onto the face of the wood, linen laid and brushed down, excess linen trimmed from the outside edges of the frame, diagonal cuts and removal of center-piece linen, turned with hot glue. Two further steps should be explained about covering a liner: the linen is turned into the rabbet and will have to be trimmed after the glue has set somewhat. With a razor blade the linen is cut away at the edge of the rabbet, working from center to corner, right and left (this avoids lifting the fabric from the corners). By pulling this fabric loose in an upward motion, one avoids disturbing the fabric already glued to the rabbet.

Fortunate indeed is the designer who knows he is backed by expert crafts-men. Just as the most skillful mat cutter and finisher can be sold out by a poor designer, the reverse is also true. It is impossible to separate good crafts-manship from good design and still come up with effective and tasteful framing.

The discussion of mats has been based so far on hand-cut mats, and this is as it should be since we are talking throughout the book about craftsman-ship. It is only fair to mention, however, that there are available on the market four or more mechanical mat cutters, one small enough to be held in the palm of the hand, others up to table size, and starting from seven or eight dollars up in price. Way up.

The mechanical mat cutting devices make it possible for an amateur to go into the picture framing business, and this is good because we all need more competition. Nothing is better for business than the opening of a new shop next door or across the street.

Elaborate claims have been made that any amateur can learn to cut pro-fessional mats within an hour after he starts practicing with these devices, but we maintain that the operator still has to know something about cutting mats before he can stack his work up against that of the professional who cuts mats by hand. We are also inclined to think that some of the fancy mats with inserts, and certainly those with multiple openings (including rectangles, ovals, and squares) would be more trouble than they were worth if cut on machines. Perhaps the biggest drawback to a mat cutting device is the danger of losing good and treasured help; a mat cutter who is proud of his craft would probably quit his job before he would consent to using a machine.

The circle- and oval-cutting machine is another story. With some rather complicated adjustments, it cuts circles and ovals with great accuracy, but it is priced clear out of reach of the amateur, and a professional framer has to be sure of a large demand for circles and ovals before he invests in such a machine, even if he is able to obtain a used one.

5 MOUNTING

THE term mount and lacquer is so common in the trade that we describe it on the order form as M&L. Actually, to mount is simply to affix a loose piece of paper to a firmer background for a more professional look and for ease in handling; to lacquer is to shoot two or more coats of clear spray lacquer onto the print to give it lifetime protection from dirt, grease, smoke, and light. A subject protected by lacquer may be framed without glass.

When framing a reproduction, we treat it as if it were the original. Thus, if the original was an oil painting, we would mount and lacquer the reproduction, and frame it without glass, as an oil painting is not glazed. If the original is a watercolor, we frame with glass (although the piece should be mounted) but there are certain exceptions. If the framed picture is to hang in a toddler's room, the hallway of a busy school, a hospital corridor, or any other area of activity where a safety factor is involved, it is wise to substitute lacquer for glass.

Prints are usually reproduced on the whitest of white paper, and it is a fallacy to suppose that any of the white should show around the picture. The print may be mounted to the full size of the paper, but then it is trimmed (if it is to be framed as an oil painting, with liners), or the white border covered by a fillet and mat. To show white around the borders simply proves that the reproduction is a reproduction, and no esthetic purpose is served by not covering it up.

Mounting falls into three categories: dry mount, adhesive mount, and wet mount. Adhesive mounting is sometimes called glue mounting, but the term is misleading. Glue, defined in the strictest sense, is a gelatinous substance derived from animal tissues. It can be made from bones, hides, hooves, or even from fish meal. The term glue has become a catchall for all kinds of adhesives from vegetable glue to plastics. The adhesive most used in our shop, Yes glue, is a vegetable-based paste that can be thinned with water.

DRY MOUNTING

The dry-mount process is generally used on photographs, certificates, small prints, citations of one sort or another, magazine covers, and occasionally fabrics. Standard prints, posters, and silk-screen prints in good condition are mounted with adhesives.

A dry-mount press is almost as indispensable to a framer as it is to a photographer, although dry mounting may be done (less handily) with an electric iron. Special dry-mounting tissue is made of plastic that melts upon the application of heat. Thus dry-mounting consists of cutting tissue and mat board to the size of the subject, affixing tissue to mat board in a couple of places with a warm tacking iron, then placing subject, tissue, and board into the press and drawing the platen of the heated press down for a few seconds.

Colored photographs must be dry mounted with special care as the emulsions are softer and frequently less set than on black-and-whites. If a colored photograph is placed in the press, covered with paper, and the press closed for fifteen seconds, there is a good chance that the protective paper will stick to the emulsion, and the framer faces disaster. This trap can be avoided with planned timing: instead of allowing an uninterrupted fifteen seconds to elapse, the process should be accomplished in five doses of pressure—one, then two, three, four, and five, for a total of fifteen seconds, the press being lifted after each interval to allow the photograph to take a deep breath.

Most certificates, documents, and photographs should be dry mounted to ensure lifetime flatness. Changes in atmosphere may cause future buckling and bulging of the paper, so the job may as well be done right in the first place. An exception is sheepskin parchment, which is no longer available. When we do get a subject printed on it, we urge the customer to accept it in

56

its three-dimensional state. The parchment itself is not valuable, but there is a certain prestige attached to owning a document printed on it.

The largest dry-mount press is 26 by 32 inches, but larger subjects may be handled in sections, starting from the center and working out, to compensate for any stretch in the paper.

ADHESIVE MOUNTING

Mounting with adhesives is somewhat more complicated as it involves a wider choice of backing materials and a number of different adhesives. The framer must "read" the subject and decide what method and material are best to use. The reason for mounting, again, is to give the subject a professional look, to repair temporary or long-term flaws, and to make for easier handling. Temporary flaws, such as one-time folding, can be completely removed by mounting; in many cases if the paper has been broken, minor cracks may be corrected by the judicious use of colored pencils.

Original graphics are never mounted because collectors of graphic art want an artwork to remain loose for handling in the marketplace. The intrinsic value of an original graphic is destroyed or at least vastly reduced when it is mounted. If the collector is sure he will never want to sell, and he would rather have the graphic mounted, an exception may be made. (Another notable exception is a piece that has been so badly damaged that its intrinsic value has already been destroyed, and mounting is all that will save it.)

The choice of mounting a temple rubbing or not is a decision that must be made by the customer. For some, the irregular, "wivvery" * look of the mulberry paper constitutes much of the charm of a rubbing; others want the piece to lie perfectly flat. The point is that the framer will save himself the nuisance of doing the job over by remembering to ask the customer his preference. Inasmuch as temple rubbings are a fairly inexpensive tourist item, little consideration need be given to their intrinsic value.

WET MOUNTING

The wet-mount process, highly specialized and sometimes complicated, is reserved for those pieces that have been badly damaged through folding and refolding, having been sat on, or mailed in an inadequate tube. This involves forcing the paper to stretch to its fullest extent, then letting it shrink; due to the shrinking, most flaws miraculously disappear. The theory behind the wet-mounting process is based on the fact that paper has two little-known qualities: it has a grain, the same as wood, and it stretches when wetted, the on-grain measurement remaining the same. A piece of newspaper tears per-

* *Word coined by Eric Knight,* The Flying Yorkshireman *(New York: Harper and Brothers. 1927).*

fectly straight parallel to the column of print, but tears unevenly at right angles to the column. When laid onto a piece of glass and wetted with a sponge, newspaper will stretch by a full inch at a right angle to the columns. Kraft paper's grain runs the length of the roll and stretches across its width. We know this to be true of newsprint and kraft paper, but there is no way of knowing ahead of time where the stretch will occur on a print, an old map, a document, or any other paper. Obviously one isn't going to tear a subject with which one has been entrusted to determine in which direction it will stretch, so one must mount the subject first and measure for framing when it has dried.

Mount boards come in a variety of weight, thickness, size, rigidity, and porosity. The two most common backings are temlock and upson board. Both come in 4- by 8-foot sheets. Temlock is $3/8$-inch thick and is rigid but somewhat porous—a refined cellulose wallboard. Upson board is $3/16$-inch thick and is quite rigid; it doesn't accept pins and thumbtacks the way temlock does. Regular mat board is used for backing, as are double-thick mat board and illustration board. Masonite, chipboard, and drywall plaster board are also available, but we find them too heavy to be practical. An excellent board has recently been introduced to the trade: available in 4- by 8-foot sheets, it is fairly rigid but unbelievably light in weight as it is made of $3/16$-inch Styrofoam, covered on both sides with white paper. It is expensive, but since it can easily be cut with one slice of a mat knife, it saves time and labor. A further advantage is that, because of its light weight, it can be used by one person to mount extremely large pieces that normally require handling by two pairs of hands.

Temlock provides an ideal background for maps, charts, and bulletin boards when pins or thumbtacks are to be used. Upson board, heavier in weight and more rigid, serves one unique, major, indispensable purpose: its edges may be cut on a bevel to show a smooth, $1/4$-inch surface: this may be painted with acrylic colors, the colored border serving as the finishing touch so no frame need be used. To date we have found no better way of handling posters, postcards, souvenir prints, and other decorative items that might be considered temporary or of passing interest. (This was a happy discovery, made by chance when we were looking for an easier way of trimming upson board, which requires at least six cuts with the mat knife to go through "on the straight." The answer, as it happened, lay in cutting on a bevel. If mat board is easier to cut on the bevel, why not upson board? So there we were with a good sharp border that must be good for something other than covering with a frame. Acrylics, mixed to match a color in the poster, seemed to be the answer, but it would take a steady hand. Then we realized that if the subject were mounted and lacquered and *then* the bevel cut, any paint spills could be easily removed from the lacquered surface. By the simple process

58

of reversing a procedure—mount, lacquer, and trim rather than mount, trim, and lacquer—a whole new aspect of framing has been discovered.)

Various types of wet adhesives are used in mounting, depending upon the paper on which the subject is printed. Most frequently used is Yes glue, a vegetable adhesive that, even when heavily diluted with water, does not shrink paper or warp mount board. White glue (marketed under a variety of trade names) is virtually a liquid plastic, and while it is occasionally used for mounting, its ideal employment is in joining frames. The grain pastes, wheat and rice, are used in wet mounting principally *because* they stretch the paper. Rice paste is somewhat more refined than wheat paste and is therefore indispensable for mounting delicate fabrics and fragile papers, such as an old newspaper or an Oriental print. It should be mentioned at this point that rubber cement has no place on the framer's adhesives shelf; it is composed of latex dissolved in benzine (and tacks only because of the benzine), and is considered an unsuitable product because of its temporary nature in a business that requires permanency.

The amateur can run into a lot of trouble by trying to do his own mounting, again because he is limited by improper or inadequate tools and workspace. A 4- by 8-foot worktable at a comfortable height is ideal, although it may be smaller. Brushes and rollers are part of the tools; three or four types of adhesives are advisable. The brush he uses for laying fabric will not do for spreading glue as it must be kept dry and clean. It is highly desirable to have a piece of plate glass for pressing mounted pieces, and it is the ideal surface for cutting mats. Most glass companies will be glad to sell a piece of "salvage plate," the glass recovered and saved when they replace a store window or an office door.

The actual job of mounting begins with measuring the subject and cutting suitable mount board to about two inches beyond the edges of the paper. Large boards are cut with the jigsaw; smaller ones with a mat knife. Next Yes glue, usually diluted for easier spreading, is applied to the back of the subject with a small trim roller. When an entirely even coat of glue has been attained, the print is laid onto the mount board, matching the corners to the pre-marked measurements, and smoothed carefully with the palms of the hands and again with a hard rubber brayer or roller to remove all bubbles. The mounted piece is then covered with a piece of plate glass, weighted at intervals over the face of the glass, and set aside to dry. (This is where "the stamina of a bricklayer" comes in: weights are heavy, and juggling large pieces of plate glass takes muscle.

It should be emphasized that glue is applied to the back of the print rather than to the face of the mounting board, as the intent is to impregnate the paper with adhesive. Irregular adhesion, causing bubbling and buckling, is sure to result if this procedure isn't followed.

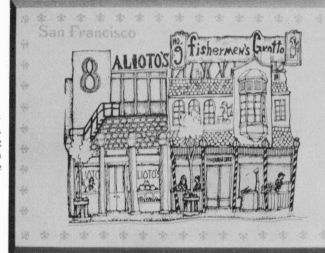

Three postcards mounted on upson board with the bevel colored. These were subsequently hung on a length of velvet ribbon from an ornamental brass ring at the top.

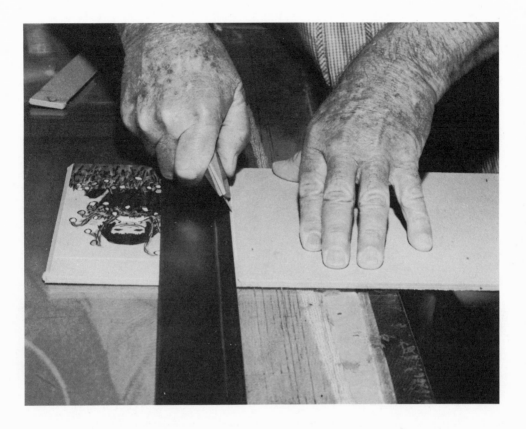

A greeting card has been mounted on upson board, and the edges are being cut on a bevel. The card will be lacquered and the angled edge will be colored with an acrylic paint.

The wet-mounting process involves an old paperhanger's trick that makes it possible for an oversized subject to be handled by only one pair of hands. First the piece is measured precisely and its dimensions written on a piece of mounting board cut roughly two inches larger all around. Paperhangers' paste is then applied to the back of the piece to be mounted, using a $3\frac{1}{2}$-inch brush that holds plenty of paste, stroking in all directions until an even coat covers. As the paper soaks up the moisture, it buckles and bubbles, but it ultimately soaks up evenly and will, when dry, lie perfectly flat. (The soaking-in process sometimes takes a while, allowing time to go do something else.)

One-third of the right side of the paper is folded onto the center third, paste touching paste. This top fold gives one a dry surface to rest on the mounting board while the exposed pasted portion—a third—is worked on. The right hand now lifts the folded portion and, turning it over, brings the pasted portion in contact with the mount board. This is smoothed down with a paperhanger's brush, thoroughly and painstakingly, until no bubbles show. There is plenty of time as grain pastes remain tacky for a long time. The remaining two-thirds are now separated and placed in contact with the board and smoothed with the brush. At this point the subject is re-measured to determine how the grain runs, remembering that it will have stretched *across* the grain, the on-grain measurement remaining the same.

Because of the shrinkage of the mounted piece, the mount board is bound to buckle and bow, so the next step is to countermount, to ensure against a bending of the background. Kraft paper, which stretches across its width, is cut to the size of the subject, matching the stretched dimension of the subject. Paste is applied to the kraft paper and rolled onto the back of the mount board. The counter-shrinkage thus pulls the background into a flat position. From now on, it is the same routine: plate glass, weights, and a twenty-four hour (or longer) wait for the subject to dry. The wet-mounting process produces some startling results. Flaws that seemed to be irreparable are shrunk right out of existence.

These products and processes have proved successful over a number of years; however, the professional framer is constantly on the look-out for new products and methods that will give him a chance to do a better job, more quickly and more easily.

CANVASES

When a canvas has hung too long in its frame without occasional attention to its condition, it can become so fragile and brittle that cleaning and re-stretching could easily ruin it. In this case the old canvas needs to be mounted on new canvas, the latter taking the brunt of stretching. If the painting is whole—no rips, tears, or thin spots—it is placed face down on glass and a good thick coating of Yes glue is applied. It is set aside while a somewhat

Glue is applied to the back of the print with a small trim roller.

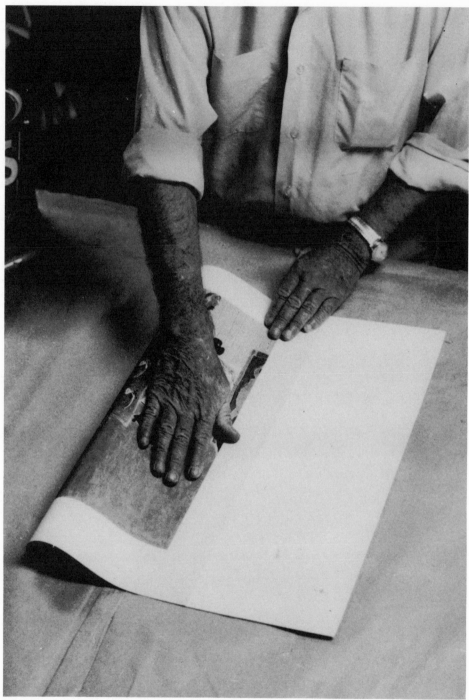

One-third of the right side of the paper is folded onto the center third, paste touching paste. This top fold gives one a dry surface to rest on the mounting board while the exposed pasted portion is worked on.

The right hand lifts the folded portion and, turning it over, brings the pasted portion in contact with the mount board.

The second and third thirds have been separated, and all excess glue is being wiped away with a barely damp sponge.

The entire print is firmly attached to the mount board by pressing it down with a brayer.

larger piece of good stout linen is treated in like manner. A union is now made between the two canvases, glue to glue. Working on the face of the painting, using paper as a cushion, the surface is rolled to ensure perfect contact between the two. (For this purpose a hand brayer such as is used by wood-block printers is necessary; the trim rollers for spreading glue and paste are not firm enough.) When all spots are flat, the two canvases are placed under glass and allowed to dry—twenty-four hours or more.

Damaged canvases are treated the same way, save for the necessity of plugging breaks in the canvas so that glue will not seep through. The holes or splits should be covered with masking tape; great care must be taken here as a tape with too strong a claw could lift off the old paint when it is removed, after mounting and before repair. Each piece of tape should be applied to a piece of glass or marble and removed repeatedly at least ten times, or until most of the adhesive quality is gone. Now the tape may be safely applied to holes and breaks in the canvas and the mounting may proceed. When the drying process has been completed, the tapes may be removed, the painting cleaned, the rips and tears carefully covered over with new oil paint, the painting varnished and put back into its frame.

Removing the tack from masking tape is also advisable when hanging a picture on a painted or plaster wall. A small square of tape applied to the area into which the nail is to be driven helps to prevent cracking the plaster; however, if the tape isn't "de-clawed" somewhat, it could take plaster and paint with it when it is removed.

6 FITTING

WE are inclined to sigh when we are asked, "Can you just sort of slip the picture into the frame while I wait?"

Fitting is a major skill, and a seasoned fitter is as indispensable to the framer as his finisher, his mat cutter, or his designer. The following steps are required to put a picture together, whether it be an 8- by 10-inch certificate, a large oil painting, or a complicated shadow box: When the frame is ready, the fitter, working from the order sheet, locates the subject and the components of the design—mat, fillet, liner, insert—and checks everything for size, condition, and other specifications. Then the subject is dry mounted, wet mounted, stretched, or stapled—whatever has to be done to make it look professional. If glass is to be used, the proper-sized glass is removed from the box, checked for flaws, cut to size and cleaned on both sides. The subject is brushed to remove dust or specks that will show up as fish—another brushing may be necessary. Now the frame is put onto the glass (another check)

69

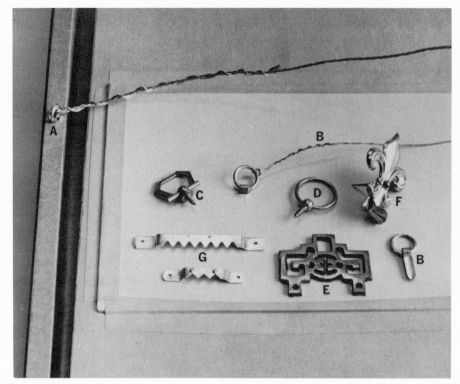

Hanging devices:

A. Standard screw eyes and wire.

B. Passe partout rings and wire for hanging posters or other unframed pieces. The ring is inserted into a slit in mat board, spread, and anchored with a bit of masking tape. The area is spread with hot glue, and fastened to the poster. Reinforcing masking tape is attached to the four sides.

C, D, E. Ornamental hangers that attach to the tops of frames.

F. Ornamental hanger.

G. Sawtooth hangers, which are nailed to the top center of a frame.

The quickest and easiest way to fit a subject into a 3-D frame is to attach screw eyes, at appropriate spaces, on the inside of the frame; then attach a screw through the eye of the screw eye.

and turned over. Unless the subject is an oil painting, double-faced corrugated backing is cut to the size of the glass (which is also the rabbet size) and with the backing in place, everything is tack-pointed or nailed into the frame. Hot glue is applied to the back of the frame and butcher's paper stretched across the entire back. Holding a single-edged razor blade in such a way that the thumb and alternately the first finger act as a guide along the edge of the frame, the fitter removes the excess paper, and any extra glue is wiped away. Proper size screw eyes are selected, brushed lightly against a piece of beeswax (to prevent drying the wood, loosening the screw eye) and screwed into holes that have been started with an awl. Proper weight wire is threaded through the screw eye on the right, pulled across the back of the frame through the left-side screw eye, wound around the shank and twisted around the cross wire. The wire is now cut from the bolt at the right side, secured to the screw eye, and wound back along the wire. If the frame is an oiled wood, with no covering finish, the nail holes in the sides of the frame are plugged with wax, non-slip pads are attached to the lower back corners of the frame, and the label glued on. When mats and fillets are involved, and glass size is, say, 30 by 40 inches, it becomes apparent that there is no such thing as "sort of slipping the picture into the frame."

In the case of an oil painting, a liner has to be covered, the liners are nailed to each other, then nailed into the frame, and the painting nailed into the innermost liner. Butcher's paper is glued only to the edge of the stretcher bars, and no double-faced corrugated backing is used. This is because a canvas must be allowed to breathe.

Fitting is a good job for an artist or art student who needs a little money to get along and won't feel too bad about leaving the job on short notice. It is a job that can be taken from town to town, and an experienced fitter has no trouble finding work in a new town within a day or two, particularly if he has developed another skill. The first thing the novice learns is glass cutting, and then he quickly moves into covering mats and liners, and even to joinery and cutting mats.

The novice fitter would not be qualified to put a shadow box together, and indeed some shadow boxes require so much special engineering that it sometimes takes two or three heads several days of working together to decide how some boxes will go together. (Cases in point: two Japanese Samurai swords the customer wants to be able to take out and oil once a month; a French fan in a fan case, to be used in an open room divider—two pieces of glass, one color of velvet on one side, another on the other; a Wedgwood porcelain clock face in an elaborate frame with an opening in the back to make the "works" available.) Each fitting job presents its own problem, whether it be taking a fly speck from a certificate or covering a 17-opening mat with black velvet; but this is why it is happy work and why a good fitter will stay with the same job year after year.

71

While stitcheries have recently come to represent a fairly routine area of framing, they are anything but routine when it comes to fitting, and are probably as responsible for almost as much blue air around the fitting table as is caused by black velvet and shadow boxes.

Needlepoints have a way of working out of square, and needlepoint workers have a way of thinking that the framer can easily pull the work back into square simply by putting a frame on it. The wool yarn has a tendency to pull the background linen in the same way that watercolor distorts paper. The only sure way to pull a needlepoint back into some semblance of square is to staple it to a firm background (wood) and dampen it, hoping that when it dries and shrinks, it will conform to the borders that were set for it. If the fitter is given only half an inch of linen background to work with, he might as well forget ever being able to square it back.

Stitcheries with a border stitch also present a major problem, and for the same reason—the thread distorts the background material. The needleworker may be proud of the evenness of the border, but as soon as we lay the straight edge of a mat or frame against it, it shows up uneven, and there is nothing we can do to square it. Here again, however, if the worker has left enough border around the work so that we can put the mat opening or the frame two or more inches outside the border, the uneven border will be lost in space, as is the uneven plate mark on an etching or engraving.

Stitcheries worked on burlap or some other stretchy material pose few problems, as the background stretches with the stitchery and can easily be squared into line. This is done exactly as a canvas is stretched, though a flat pine liner can be used instead of the more expensive stretcher bars. In the case of burlap or a similar porous material, it is wise to give the liner a coat of lacquer the same color as the burlap so that the light, raw wood doesn't show through.

GLASS

The mere mention of glass arouses some interesting reactions. Some customers refuse to use anything but non-reflecting glass, others consider it a dirty word, and still others are adamant against using glass at all, regardless of the medium. The purpose of glass, of course, is to protect the subject from the deteriorating effects of dirt, grease, smoke, moths, and other natural enemies. It is thus almost mandatory to glaze any subject but oil paintings (protected by varnish), lithographs (protected by spray lacquer), ceramics, copper enamels, wood and metal sculptures, and other pieces whose structure serves as their own protection. Some customers are so opposed to the use of glass that they will insist on mounting a watercolor or even a pastel rather than glaze it.

Glass is one of the most flexible products we have. It can be bent to a large degree without breaking and then returned to its original state, whereas a rubber band may be flexed to its fullest length, but it will be a little longer after each stretching.

Non-reflecting glass is a most welcome addition to the trade.* Due to a special process by which it is lightly etched in an acid bath, it presents a surface that bounces back virtually no reflection, whereas regular picture glass serves more nearly as a mirror in a sunny room or a brightly lighted area. Thus non-reflecting glass has served as an enormous boon to the business, as it provides an alternative to glass where bright light detracts from a picture's purpose and effectiveness. Known as non-glare, NG, and by any of a number of trade names, non-reflecting glass has a few drawbacks in spite of its definite advantages. It doesn't work on every subject because it tends to distort colors, deaden blacks, and to reduce the whiteness of whites, even when it is set directly onto the subject. The farther it is removed from the subject, the more distortion takes place; thus printing becomes difficult to read at ½ inch and is entirely undecipherable at 2 inches. (It obviously cannot be used on shadow boxes.) Usually non-reflecting glass can be used successfully over a mat and fillet; in the case of a brilliant watercolor or an acrylic, it can even sometimes be used with a double fillet and mat.

Another objection to the indiscriminate use of non-reflecting glass is a somewhat subtle one—it tends to make an original piece of art look like a reproduction. This is particularly true of watercolors and old etchings or engravings. Conversely, using regular glass on a reproduction print can subtly suggest that it is an original.

Price is another item in the choice between the two types of glass. Non-reflecting glass is about twice as costly as regular glass; we can even go a step further and mention that it indicates a modicum of luxury not only when used in a home or office, but also when used on a gift.

In many instances sheer practicality dictates the decision to use glass or not. As a maintenance factor, glass-cleaning time may be saved if pictures in bathrooms and kitchens are protected from steam and grease by the mount-and-lacquer process. As a price factor, the cost of mounting and lacquering usually just about equals the cost of glass. Weight also plays a part in the pro-or-con decision on glass. The larger the glass, obviously, the sturdier the frame needs to be. If a customer prefers a narrow frame (½ inch) on a 17- by 39-inch poster, he is going to have to do without glass or pay substantially more for specially engineered fitting. Single-strength picture glass weighs about thirteen ounces per square foot; one light of glass size 30 by 40 weighs between seven and eight pounds, which brings up not only

---

* *Considerable research has unearthed a rather startling bit of non-information: no one, even executives in the glass industry, seems to know exactly when non-glare glass first hit the market. Opinions vary within a range of ten years—from 1945 to 1955. However, 1945 seems somewhat too far removed, as the process doesn't seem to have been developed during World War II.*

the question of the weight of a framed picture and the difficulty of handling it during fitting and hanging, but also the strain that it might put on a wall.

Framing a subject between two pieces of glass is sometimes necessary if both sides are important to the customer. In this instance, either two frames are used, back to back, or shims are inserted into the back of the frame. Framing between two pieces of glass larger than the subject, so that the glass is an extension instead of a mat, constitutes a contrivance that serves no practical purpose, and we tend to discourage the customer who requests it. In the first place, there are few wall coverings that can serve as a more effective complement to a picture than a well-chosen mat. Further, a second piece of glass produces impractical extra weight. Finally, the extra cost of fitting, due to shims and the extra care that needs to be taken to avoid breaking the glass—to say nothing of cleaning the two—just isn't compatible with a job that is not esthetically worth it.

Picture glass is used by most framers because it is thinner than window glass ($\frac{1}{16}$-inch thick) and hence lighter in weight and easier to cut. It is available in stock sizes up to 36 by 48 inches, which is also the maximum size of non-reflecting glass. Sizes over 38 by 50 must be cut from double-strength window glass, which goes to 52 by 68, and obviously would require the sturdiest kind of a frame. The next weight, which we never use, is called crystal and comes in thicknesses of $\frac{3}{16}$ and $\frac{7}{32}$ inch. Finally, plate glass (such as is used in store windows and sliding doors) is $\frac{1}{4}$ and $\frac{1}{2}$ inch thick. Quarter-inch plate is as heavy as we need for weighting.

Glass is cut by the arm, not the hand. The hand, of course, holds the glass cutting tool, but the elbow is kept stiff, and the cut is made by backing away as the tool moves down the glass. The glass cutter is held as a pencil is held, but in a more upright position and at a true right angle to the surface of the glass.

The wheel of the glass cutter is pressed onto the glass, the left hand holding the glass securely with the frame. The cut must be made in one continuous motion. The idea is to break the surface of the glass along the full length of the cut, and the excess may then be broken off with the fingers. If the extra glass is narrow, say $\frac{1}{4}$-inch, it may be tapped off with the end of the glass cutter or broken off clean with a pair of pliers.

The best way to tell if the cut is clean is by sound. A good steady hiss means a clean cut; a series of staccato "dots" indicates that the tool should be sharpened or that a little less pressure should be applied.

The easiest method is to cut directly to the frame. The frame is laid face down on the table, the upper left corner of the glass resting in the rabbet of the corresponding corner of the frame. The cut is made and the excess glass broken off. Then the frame is turned to the shorter side and the second cut made. When the excess glass is tapped or broken off, the glass falls into the frame with a satisfying plop.

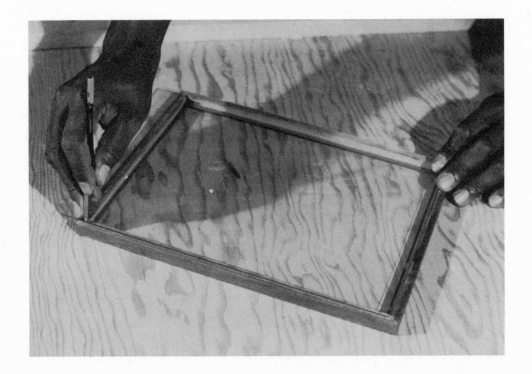

Glass is most easily cut against the frame. The glass cutting tool is held much as one holds a pencil.

When the cut is completed, the waste segment of glass is broken off by the fingers. Notches on the end of the tool can be used for breaking chipped glass, if the cut was not smooth and true.

Glass may also be cut against the edge of a piece of mat board, or to penciled lines on a sheet of paper.

A little practice with a new glass cutting tool, making cuts on a piece of 8- by 10-inch glass, will make a glass cutter of almost any amateur within a few minutes. Even a seasoned fitter, however, when he takes an $\frac{1}{8}$-inch sliver off the long side of a 30 by 40 glass, shows it around the shop.

Cutting glass for circular and oval frames is a more complicated procedure. Since the secret of successful glass cutting lies in making a continuous cut, it obviously takes a steady hand and some skillful shifting to cut glass on an arc instead of on a straight line.

Most fitters prefer to break the surface of the glass against the frame, but sometimes the frame is not available, in which case the following procedure is highly successful. A piece of mat board is scribed with a compass and marked with soft pencil to the desired size. Then a rectangular piece of glass is attached to the mat board with pressure-sensitive tape, thus making it possible to turn the pattern and the glass with the left (or non-cutting) hand, while the right hand continues the cut.

When the surface of the glass has been broken, straight lines are scribed with the glass-cutting tool, tangentially to the circle. The glass is removed from the pattern board and placed cut side down and taps are made on the wedges until the cuts open up. The wedge-shaped pieces now either fall away or may be broken off with the fingers.

Plexiglas is not really recommended as a substitute for glass. When in thin, rollable sheets, there is no way of making it lie absolutely flat, and in thicker sheets it carries a certain amount of opacity, scratches easily, gathers dust, and is almost prohibitively expensive.

7 CUT-AND-JOIN

JOINERY—a beautiful word, which the skill of cut-and-join deserves—is one phase of picture framing that is sometimes taught at trade schools and can therefore be learned outside of a frame shop. The amateur woodworker can easily adjust his skill to making frames if he has the proper tools, a working knowledge of mathematics, an understanding of pitfalls to be encountered, and a preconceived notion of what the finished product is to look like.

The finished frame should be joined in such a way that the corners match exactly at both the outside and rabbet edges, as well as across the top or face of the moulding. This can be accomplished only if the moulding is cut precisely on a 45-degree angle, with no split wood, and properly glued and nailed. Obviously tools must be sharp and measurements accurate, equipment securely in place, and the hand steady.

Large, busy, factory-type shops are usually equipped with more than one cutting device; smaller shops are usually limited to one. The radial saw and the table or bench saw are the most accurate and versatile, although many shops use a chopper, operated by hand, foot, or power. Radial and bench saws cut the moulding from back to rabbet; choppers chop down on the face of the moulding. The saws may be adjusted to cut a rabbet on raw lumber, to rip mouldings to a narrower width, and to cut other than 45-degree angles. Choppers cut mouldings only up to 4 inches in width and are inclined to chip a gesso-coated or compo moulding, although the skill of the operator is often a factor. The advantage to a chopper lies in economizing on moulding: it cuts two facing 45-degree angles at one chop, resulting in waste of only the resulting triangle. It takes some doing to keep a chopper in proper alignment, but it is also a less expensive piece of equipment than either of the saws, takes up a lot less room, and at the same time creates much less sawdust.

Saw blades and chopper blades must, of course, be kept sharp, and are sent out to professional sharpeners as often as the volume of work necessitates.

A power jig is almost a must for cutting upson board and other heavy mount boards.

A hand saw and mitre box are hardly considered professional equipment, yet at the same time are entirely adequate for the amateur. If it is at all possible, the mitre box should be permanently anchored to a work bench, since stability makes for greater accuracy.

Bench saws and radial saws differ principally in the way they are mounted. The blade of a bench saw protrudes through the top of a worktable, and moulding is fed into it across the table top. The radial saw is suspended from a turret-arm, and moulding is cut by drawing the blade across the moulding.

A mitre vise and a stationary drill are bolted to a bench secured to the floor in concrete, making for the important stability mentioned above. A power hand drill is suspended within easy reach of the joiner for drilling small holes.

The joiner reads the work sheet, lays out the proper moulding, and promptly makes some automatic calculations. Let's say the order calls for a 16 by 20 frame cut from $\frac{1}{2}$-inch stock. First he adds $\frac{1}{8}$ inch to allow for a little play around the glass; if the frame is cut to the exact dimension of 16 by 20, a piece of 16 by 20 glass won't slide easily into the rabbet. Next he adds twice the width of the frame—in this instance 1 inch—to compensate for loss of moulding in the mitre. To cut a 16 by 20 frame, then, his markings on the outer edge of the moulding will be made at $17\frac{1}{8}$ and at $21\frac{1}{8}$. This is because he makes the cut from the back edge of the moulding into the rabbet. When the frame is joined, the rabbet measurement will read $16\frac{1}{8}$ by $20\frac{1}{8}$.

Once in a while an order calls for a sight measurement. This means that the customer wants all the picture to show, with nothing hidden under the rabbet. (Photographs, Christmas cards, and etchings on metallic papers usually fall into this category.) In this case the joiner doesn't make the ⅛-inch adjustment to the rabbet measurement.

The joiner may be faced with five orders on one order sheet reading:

2 — 8 × 10	½″ flat black	certificates
1 — 20 × 23½	— walnut borghese, dark oil	watercolor
1 — 4½ × 7½	— 673 — green velvet	
	+ gold stem	medals
1 — 17 × 18	⅜ flat gold	oil on canvas
	+ 587 — 2½″ Belgian linen	
	+ walnut stem — teak	
1 — 11 × 14	½″ gold top walnut	photograph

The third and fourth items represent another type of calculation; 673 is a functional liner for a shadow box and is covered in velvet, which means that

A length of moulding is selected and the measurement marked out by pencil. Allowance has been made, at the 10-inch marking, for the width of the frame. To permit extra "play" around the glass, ¼-inch (two ⅛s) is allowed beyond the 1-inch mark.

the gold stem should be cut $\frac{1}{4}$ inch larger to allow for the thickness of velvet, plus the calculation he has already made for the width of the second frame. The fourth line involves two liners, the second to be covered in linen; thus another allowance for the thickness of linen has to be figured before the outside frame is cut. This isn't really as complicated as it seems, as such figurings become virtually automatic to a good cut-and-join man.

Other alterations that the joiner may sometimes have to calculate are: an extra allowance for a deep-rabbeted moulding (some have a $\frac{1}{2}$-inch rabbet), a liner covered in fabric, or a liner that will be fitted into a three-dimensional or floating frame, in which case the fabric must be turned over the outside edge of the liner, thus requiring a somewhat larger frame.

A good joiner usually measures the subject and doublechecks the designer's measurements. Many times a subject, such as an oil painting or something painted on Masonite, is off by as much as an $\frac{1}{8}$ inch on one side, so the joiner must make an allowance for a tight fit on one end and a loose fit on the other. When precision is the watchword, $\frac{1}{16}$ inch means a lot.

Most joiners lay out their orders, take all their measurements, and do all the cutting before they start to join. This certainly is an economy from the standpoint of time. Cutting and joining one frame at a time is slow, tedious, and time-consuming.

Joining begins by drilling holes at the left-hand end of all four pieces of moulding, two for narrow frames, three or more for larger frames. The hand drill is used to make holes just smaller than the brads or nails that will be used to join the frame. (This preliminary drilling serves to keep the wood from splitting when the nail is driven.) The bench drill is used if larger nails will be required on larger, heavier mouldings. One long length of moulding is then clamped into the bench vise, the rabbet facing away from the worker, and a small amount of white glue is applied to the mitred surface, directly out of the bottle. Next a short length, with holes drilled, is butted against the long length, but overlapping by $\frac{1}{8}$ inch. Nails are inserted into the drilled holes and driven home with a tack hammer. As the nails are driven, the short length moves slightly inward to make a firm, flush joint. The nails are then countersunk with a nail set.

It is also the job of the joiner to coordinate the frame with its order number and the finish it is to receive. He writes such information on the back of the frame so the next worker in line knows what to do: "Gold leaf with antique and spatter" to the finisher; "light Belgian linen" or "lipstick red velvet" to the fitter. (This is our routine. We understand that some shops train their employees so that one person does the design, writes up the order, cuts and joins the frame, and finishes it, and also does mats, liners, and fitting. As a general rule, however, most employees are limited to two or three skills.)

82

One highly professional method of joining a frame is with a wooden spline at each corner. (This is frequently seen on Oriental frames, particularly Japanese.) Slots are cut in both ends of the lengths of moulding and a piece of matching wood driven in to make the joint. When secured with glue and clamped until the glue is dry, this type of joinery is not only handsome but extremely durable.

Unfortunately, the big frame factories, where frames are joined by machine on a production line, frequently join liners and frames by means of a metal spline. These make for somewhat inaccurate joints, and are almost impossible to take apart if a frame is to be refinished or cut down. About the only advantage to joining with a metal spline is that it is cheap, making it possible for variety stores to sell large, framed prints for $9.99.

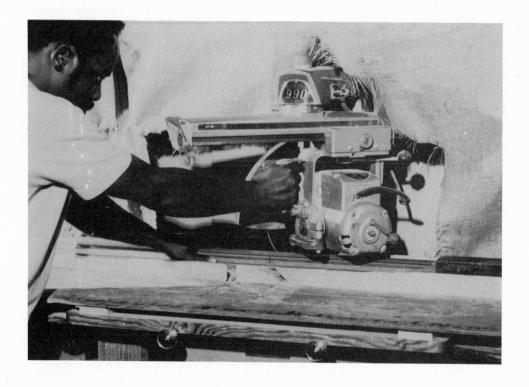

If a number of frames are to be joined at one time, they are usually measured and marked and the right-to-left cuts completed before the saw is adjusted for the left-to-right cuts. The saw is pulled through from the back of the moulding at a 45-degree angle. The burlap casing helps to contain at least some of the sawdust.

The saw has been adjusted to make a cut from left to right. A chopper makes both cuts at once.

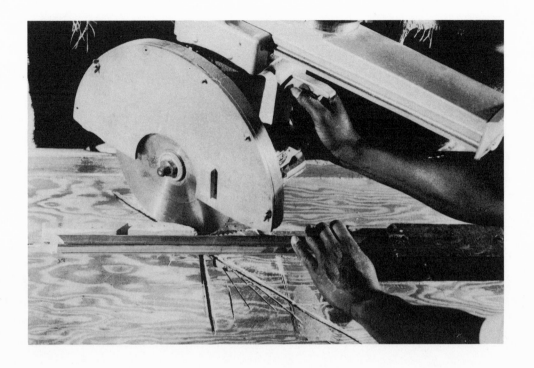

A block of solid steel holds a length of moulding stationary when the cut is made.

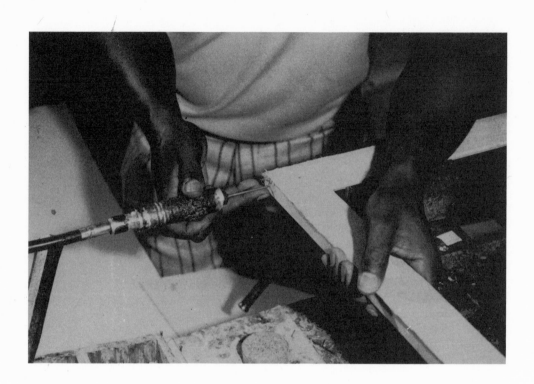

Holes are drilled just deep enough to hold the nails until they are driven home.

The nail has been brushed against the beeswax disk in the foreground and is being driven home. Liner covered in the stick was used to illustrate the way the vise-held side is backed away from the second stick. When the nail is driven in, the two joints meet in a perfect 45-degree mitre.

Kiobe corners have rounded contours that lend themselves well to the delicacy of Oriental art. *Above:* Kiobe corner—wood finish. *Below:* Kiobe corner, gold leaf with spatter.

With the advent of new adhesives, frames may be joined simply by clamping. Sets of adjustable clamps are available, packaged with a sort of reverse-style pliers, for opening the clamp while the frame is set in. Holes still need to be filled, as the clamps make a hole in each section of moulding, and we are inclined to think that the process takes somewhat longer than standard joinery.

KIOBE CORNERS

The softly rounded contours of a frame with Kiobe corners lend themselves particularly well to the delicacy of Oriental art. Oval-top moulding is most successfully used, the width depending on the size of the picture.

Moulding is cut to the specified size, and the joiner nips off each end of all four sticks, removing the mitre. When the frame is joined, each corner shows a notch, the V facing the V of the inside corner rather than repeating it. These notches are rounded off with a steel file, and the frame is grooved about halfway through its face along the mitre. The whole frame is carefully sanded, with special attention to smooth corners.

The frame can then be leafed and lightly spattered, or shot with a few coats of colored lacquer, subtle colors being preferable.

8 FINISHING

We have said that proportion, color, and the components that go next to the picture are more important than the frame itself. Also, that any type of manipulation of the frame against the picture negates the purpose of framing. We also maintain that the type of finish used on the frame makes a tremendous difference in the appearance of the finished product. Moulding of the same size and shape, finished in three different ways, can change the whole character of the picture. An oiled walnut finish is suitable for any office, home, hospital, or school; a fruitwood finish on the same frame blends it into Early American decor or softens it enough for use in a bedroom or dining area; a softly spattered borghese suggests enough elegance to use the picture in an entrance hall or as the focal center of a newly decorated living room.

Decisions regarding finishing are made at the design table between the designer and the customer (who may own the picture or may be a decorator).

Consider, then, the plight of the finisher who sometimes has to deal with a problem created from four different opinions: the designer's idea, the customer's understanding of that idea, the customer's idea (the owner's idea if a decorator is involved), and his own reaction to the picture. Thus a finisher must have not only tremendous manual skills but impeccable taste as well. He must be able to create nuances of color and antiquing that make the finished picture a complete work of art.

It has been said that a finisher should keep an exact step-by-step account of every finish that is shown on the display board, allowing for no deviation from one use of that finish to the next. But this is simply not individualized framing, and also virtually impossible to do. As a creative artist, a finisher cannot precisely repeat himself two weeks later, particularly if he has any personal interest in the picture being framed. (He may think little of the picture, but his professional pride forces him to do his creative best.)

Finishing frames involves the same tender and patient care that goes into finishing furniture, which means that preparation is of prime importance. Meticulous sanding obviously is the first step, tedious though it is. Many finishers prefer to do their own sanding in order to feel a relationship with the finished product, but this chore is frequently delegated to an all-purpose employee who may also cover liners and do some fitting. A knowledge of wood, and a feel for it is needed for good finishing work.

The frame hangs on hooks and is held lightly with the left hand while lacquer is sprayed from the gun.

The spray gun is operated off a compressor. The spray booth is ventilated so that lacquer fumes are drawn off by an electric fan.

When all four sides have been sprayed, the frame is set to dry on the drying racks. Then it is gas-sanded (fine steel wool impregnated with benzine or turpentine) to a satin-smooth surface, and sprayed again. Sometimes five or six repetitions of this process are required to achieve a flawless finish.

Wood is generally divided into two categories: hard, from the deciduous trees; soft, from the evergreens or conifers. Hardwoods give us good finishes because they have a grain that can be brought up with judicious sanding and further accentuated by the application of oil. The natural color of the wood is retained by using clear oil, or it may be darkened by using pigmented oils.

Hardwoods used for framing would therefore include poplar, cedar, birch, alder, maple, and walnut, to mention a few. Oak, teak, mahogany, fall into the category of hardwoods, but are entirely too hard to be practical for making frames. Oak was enormously popular for some years—while the supply held out—although it is hard to understand why. The wood itself is so hard that it doesn't adapt itself to subtleties of shape when run through the sticker at the planing mill. It is also impossible to finish it to look like anything but oak, and a light—almost yellow—frame polished to high gloss does absolutely nothing for any picture that we can think of. In fact, durability is about the only claim that may be made for an oak frame, and that amounts, as we have hinted rather broadly, to something of a pity.

Wormy chestnut enjoyed an enormous vogue some years ago and currently retains a certain popularity, although the wormholes are now made with drills, and little of the wood is real chestnut. During the nineteenth century chestnut was used for making furniture, but with the blight of 1863, worms made such a shambles of the chestnut groves that the wood was no longer

suitable for this purpose.* Thus a fashion for wormy chestnut had to be created in other areas, and it was widely touted as picture framing material, as well as wall paneling, staircases, newel posts, and the like. The wood was virtually useless for any other purpose and had to be sold at rock-bottom prices, and who is looking for lower prices than the picture framer? And so a fad was invented and still persists, even though there isn't anything particularly gratifying, esthetically, about a frame that has been chomped full of holes.

The softwoods—pine, spruce, and juniper—are used for liners and for lacquered or painted finishes. Easier to join and easier to sand, they are more porous than the hardwoods, so they drink up an undercoat such as Luminall or titanated shellac when a marble-smooth surface is needed. Sugar pine is undoubtedly the most widely used wood in the framing industry. Most prefinished mouldings are made from it for the reasons just mentioned, and more prefinished than unfinished mouldings are sold to framers.

Walnut and substitutes for it are currently the most popular woods for making wood-finished frames, although planing mills are always looking for other woods, particularly since American walnut is almost gone. (Real American walnut is terribly expensive for two reasons: it is scarce and getting scarcer, and the color varies so within the space of only a couple of feet from almost white to dark brown—piebald—that there is much waste when uniformity of color is a consideration. The designer should point out and the customer understand that a corner sample of walnut moulding is not representative of the color of the finished frame, but just a close approximation. Mansonia, an African walnut, provides us, on the other hand, with a wood that is fairly uniform in color and comes in lengths as long as fourteen feet.)

A power sander is used on large or wide frames, but much sanding is also done by hand, with a sanding block or with small squares of loose sandpaper. A couple of strokes with the power sander are usually enough to make the frame smooth to the touch—anyone who has refinished furniture knows that the tactile test is best—although some woods will never be completely smooth, notably birds-eye maple, whose "eyes" are as hard as rock and therefore unsuited for a leafed or lacquered finish, as the eyes cannot be sanded down to the level of the wood, and will always show through leaf or lacquer as polkadots. In its natural state, with a protective coat of clear shellac, it is one of the handsomest woods we use, particularly well suited to old-fashioned subjects.

Basically the finisher's concern is twofold: to build up the surface of the wood or to break it down. He builds up by sanding and by applying

94

* *James Thurber claimed that his grandfather's brother, Zenas, was the only human being to fall victim to the chestnut blight of '63 (or at least that is what his grandfather claimed).* "The Car We Had to Push," from My Life and Hard Times (New York: Blue Ribbon Books. 1933).

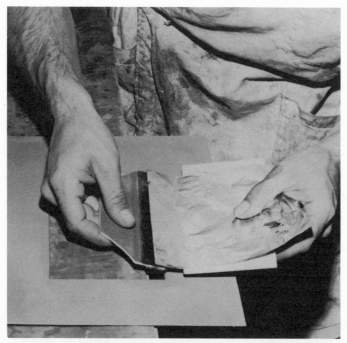

Metal leaf is lifted with a tool made of mat board covered on both sides with a strip of velvet (right hand).

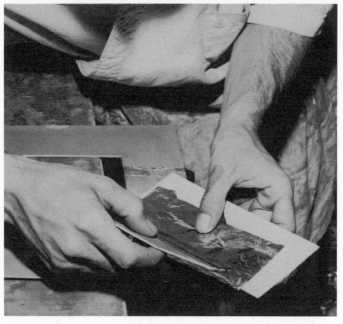

The left thumb holds the leaf in place while the right hand lifts it at the outer edge.

The leaf is smoothed onto the mat board with the velvet-covered tool.

The velvet-covered tool is moved back (from right to left) across the board, adhering the leaf to the oil-sized surface.

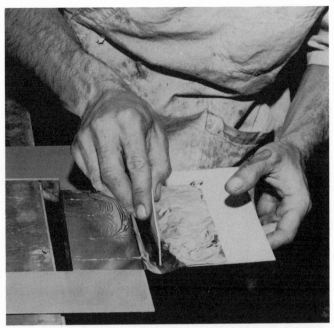

The leaf is loose at the outside edges because only about ¾-inch at the window opening has been treated with gold size. The loose leaf may be lifted and used on the rest of the fillet.

Fillet is left to dry on the drying rack.

various materials to create smooth surfaces; he breaks down with coarse sandpaper, steel wool, rasps, combs, and gouges. Carved frames are expensive because they require both processes: refined breaking down in a precise pattern with carving tools, and building up to the ultimate refinement of gold leaf.

The most comprehensive book we have seen on the subject of finishing wood is *The Art of the Painted Finish—for Furniture and Decoration,* by Isabel O'Neil (a House and Garden Book published by William Morrow and Co., in 1971). The author has described in minute and easy-to-understand detail the step-by-step processes for achieving every finish that has ever been conceived. For the technician who might care to go into finishing beyond the few basics we describe farther on, the O'Neil book is simply invaluable. Any O'Neil finish could be adapted to a picture frame, except that frame finishes need not be as durable, obviously, as furniture finishes, so the framer may use materials requiring a shorter drying time. It would be unnecessary, for instance, to add flat white paint or spar varnish to colors ground in japan; instead turpentine or benzine or paint thinner for glazes or tones over a lacquer or leaf base could be used. In other words, any furniture finish may be used on a raw picture frame, but the final sealer coat may be of a faster drying, less durable material.

It seems in order at this point to delineate the finisher's materials and to describe their uses:

FOR SURFACE PREPARATION

Water-base wood putty for filling holes and correcting blemishes (to be sanded smooth when dry).

Number 240 sandpaper for sanding wood.

Fine steel wool, 4/0, for smoothing lacquer.

Number 400 sandpaper with water for extra-smooth lacquer. (This is also known as emery cloth and may be used wet or dry, with gasoline, benzine, turpentine, or soapsuds. This technique is used in decoupage.)

UNDERCOATS

Lacquer-based white filler coat to fill grain for lacquer or leaf.

Luminall, a water-based liquid used for building up the surface for lacquer or leaf or distressed finishes.

Titanated shellac (shellac containing titanium) for the same purpose.

Color coat for leafing (yellow for gold, gray for silver, salmon for copper, yellow for multicolored leaf; red, green or black for rub-through on leafed frames.

98

FINISHING

Colored lacquers; japans; alcohol-based wood stains (non-grain-raising); stains; oils, rottenstone (a powder used over wet lacquer as an antique. It is brushed on and blown off. It must be kept on a bottom shelf! To spill it is disaster!)

SEALERS

French varnish to protect leaf from lacquer; clear lacquer to seal colored lacquers and leafs and any other finish that requires a shiny look; matte lacquer for dull finishes (flatting agent in clear lacquer).

FINISHING TOUCHES

Luminall mixed lightly with black to create a soft gray; colors in japan. Luminall stays on top of the finish and presents an opaque appearance. Japan gives a translucent finish but eats through lacquer if rubbed too hard or too much. Spatter: India ink—black, brown, brick red, dark green, etc. Amaco wood waxes for filling nailholes at final fitting. These waxes are obtainable in eight colors and eight wood finishes, as well as gold and silver.

FINISHER'S TOOLS

Finishes are applied with a surprisingly small number of tools. Cotton waste (refuse fiber from cotton mills), which looks a lot like balled-up string, is probably the commonest applicator. Lint-free sheeting is used for wiping off excess oil and lacquer. The spray gun, which operates from a tank of compressed air fed by a compressor, is in actuality an airbrush and is used the same way a brush is used. Brushes are used mostly for applying size, rottenstone, touch-ups, and color in panels. Lacquer may be brushed on, but more coats are required as well as longer drying time, to say nothing of the time it takes to use steel wool between coats. (When lacquer is brushed on, it is used thicker than when it is sprayed.) Heavy-duty rubber gloves should be considered tools, as they are used to protect the hands from many materials that are wiped on.

Prefinished mouldings need only be "cornered," which means that the finisher, using a sharp knife, pares off any irregularities at the mitred joint and dabs on a bit of colored lacquer, stain, or gold or silver wax to cover any exposed raw wood. These corners often need only to be sanded before the touch-up.

THE FINISHER'S NOTEBOOK

SIMPLEST WOOD FINISH (Light, Medium, or Dark Oils)

These are used on walnut and substitutes, canewood, maple, and any other hardwoods whose grain is enhanced by emphasizing it. Oil is applied generously to the sanded frame with cotton waste and set aside. After about ten minutes another coat of oil is applied and is wiped off immediately with cotton sheeting. The frame can be fitted as soon as the oil has set. (This is the general method; directions on the can of oil should always be read and followed.)

99

TEAK FINISH

This finish is used when black is required but lacquer would be too harsh. Black alcohol stain is applied with cotton waste and a coat of clear lacquer is sprayed on. Black japan is wiped on with waste and wiped off—carefully— with cotton sheeting. The turpentine will eat the lacquer if it is rubbed too hard. When the finish has set, another coat of clear lacquer is applied.

LACQUER FINISH

After the color has been mixed, it is thinned with lacquer thinner and the gun is tested. If lacquer comes out in little dots, it is too thick; if it runs easily, it is too thin, in which case either more lacquer is added or the finisher sprays a little faster. When the color has been applied, the frame is set aside to dry. It is then rubbed with steel wool and given a coat of clear lacquer. (Clear lacquer is used, one pint thinner to one pint lacquer.)

The airbrush produces a fan-shaped flow of color that is literally brushed onto the surface being finished. The operator starts a flow of material before the lacquer meets the frame and continues the flow past the article in a smooth, even sweep. Any hesitation will cause a build-up of lacquer, and consequently a run. Lacquer dries rapidly, so the finisher never tries to cover in one coat, applying instead several thin, quick-drying coats.

When the lacquer is dry, the finish may be further refined by using a lacquer cutting compound (fine abrasive in a water-soluble base) or extra-fine steel wool. Any mistakes, such as pile-ups, runs, lumps, or "orange peel" (the effect of too-thick lacquer) may be corrected with this so-called "gas-sanding."

Since lacquer is a light-bodied medium, finishers prefer a suction-type spray gun as opposed to a pressure-type gun. The air stream flows over the top of a tube which lifts the material out of the can.

WOOD STAINS

Colored stains, called non-grain-raising stains, are available at good paint stores. These are applied to the sanded frame with cotton waste. The color darkens as more stain is applied, so the finished color may be controlled by the number of coats the wood soaks up. Colored stains require no further finishing.

FRUITWOOD

Fruitwood, an alcohol-base stain available in many colors, is applied with cotton waste, and a coat of clear lacquer is applied as a sealer. Burnt umber in japan is next applied with cotton waste, and another coat of clear lacquer applied. This process is repeated three times: fruitwood, clear lacquer, japan, wipe; clear lacquer, steel wool, fruitwood, wipe, clear lacquer. Spatter, if

100

required, is applied at this point and sealed with another coat of clear lacquer. If no spatter is called for, the last coat of clear lacquer finishes the process. If a shinier finish is desired, a second coat of lacquer may be applied.

DRIFTWOOD

The raw, unsanded frame is distressed with gouging tools. A delicate distressing may be done with a steel comb, always working with the grain of the wood. Heavier scratches may be made with a gouge, working quickly and in rhythm lest the pattern lose continuity. Sometimes it is desirable to mix light scratching with deeper gouging. From the first step to the last, the finisher keeps in mind that the total effect of the finished frame is to look as if it were made out of old wood washed up on the beach.

Luminall may be brushed on before distressing or after heavy distressing. When the luminall is dry, more distressing may be added by using coarse steel wool. Corrections (too deep a hole, or too many) may be made with luminall at this point. The desired color coat, in japan, is applied with cotton waste. When dry, sanding with steel wool will bring through some white (luminall) as a contrast to the color, if even more distressing is desired. A fairly heavy coat of clear lacquer is applied and a quick coat of rottenstone is brushed on and blown off before the lacquer dries. Spatter, if needed, is applied at this point. The frame is set on a low rack to dry.

LEAFING

The frame is sanded and a coat of filler applied. When dry, it is sanded again and another coat of filler added. This is repeated until the surface is mirror-smooth. Colored lacquer color coat is now sprayed onto the frame, and when it is dry a generous coat of size is brushed on, care being taken that the size gets into all the corners (many compo ornaments are quite deep) and into low places in the frame. (Leaf will not adhere where size is absent.) Size is brushed on several times to ensure an even coat. When size has been built up to an even, wet surface, the finisher starts to brush it off, wiping the brush often on cotton sheeting. When the brush drags, the frame is set to one side until the size has set. (The length of time depends on how much drying agent was used in the size.) To test its readiness for leaf, the pinky, clean, is pressed into a corner. If the finger doesn't slide, the frame is ready to be leafed.

Leaf must be handled gently. It is guided into position, not dumped. Working from the inside edge of the frame, with the edge of the leaf parallel to the edge of the frame, each sheet of leaf is lifted and guided into place, then pressed down gently with the velvet-edged lifting tool. It is well not to split the leaf in low spots, and to remember that the overlapping seams should be kept straight, as they show through. A burnisher is used to press

101

the leaf down more securely. Usable excess is torn off at the outside bottom edge of the frame and set aside for patching, if necessary. When leaf has been laid on the whole frame, an absorbent cotton swab and more leaf (scraps) are used to get into corners and low spots. If the first leaf has broken, the second patching should fill it in. Cotton should be changed frequently and kept soft for getting into cracks and corners. If a low spot won't fill with leaf, two or three layers of leaf may be forced in with a cotton swab.

Excess leaf is now rubbed off with a cotton swab, to remove the overlaps when the leaf was laid. If the leaf was laid from left to right, the excess is removed from right to left; if this pattern is not followed, the leaf may lift. Any patching may be done at this point. A generous coat of French varnish is applied to protect the leaf from lacquer and is immediately sealed with a coat of clear lacquer. Spatter or antiquing is now done, and everything is sealed again.

When leafing a mat or fillet, the finisher lays the whole mat on the work-table. After each sheet of leaf is laid, he lifts the mat and presses the leaf onto the bevel. Leaf doesn't stretch; it settles.

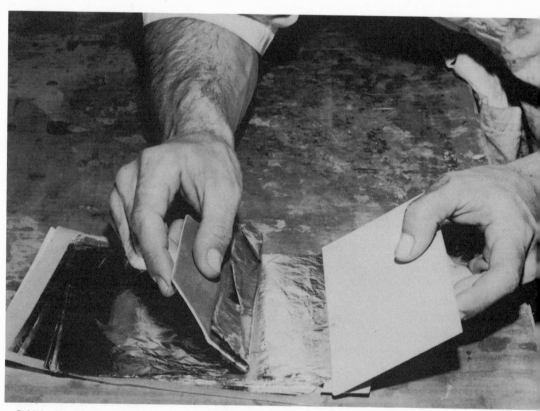

Gold leaf is lifted, using a velvet-covered mat in one hand and a guiding mat in the other.

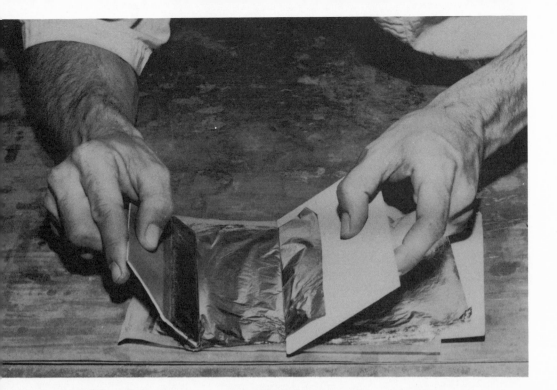

Top: The static set up by the velvet-edged matboard makes it possible to lift the other edge of the leaf with a piece of mat board and to transfer it tenderly to the subject to be leafed. Bottom: The fillet has been treated with a coat of luminall or titanated shellac, sanded to a mirror finish, and treated with gilding oil (size). When the proper tack is reached, leaf is applied as shown.

RUB-THROUGH ON LEAF

If some color is to show through the gold (or silver) leaf, the leafed surface is rubbed lightly with fine steel wool just after the excess leaf is removed. Long, even strokes are used, and the finisher stops just before the desired amount of color comes through. (Subsequent coats of clear lacquer bring up the color of the undercoat.) French varnish and clear lacquer are applied, and any finishing touches put on.

CRACKLE

To create a crackle finish on all or part of a frame, such as a raised lip or a flat panel, the following procedure is followed: after the filler coats have been properly built up, a coat of clear lacquer is applied. If a fine crackle is desired, the lacquer should be the highest gloss; the more matte the lacquer, the wider the crackle. Clear or white crackle (available at good paint stores) is sprayed or brushed onto the surface and allowed to dry—crackle. The color coat is applied and then the leaf.

BORGHESE

The frame is prepared as for any leaf, then silver leaf is laid in the same manner as gold. Raw Sienna japan is wiped on with cotton waste and most of it wiped off, for just a hint of color. A delicate spatter is added and the frame (or mat) sprayed with clear lacquer.

ANTIQUING

Slightly grayed luminall is applied with cotton waste to the surface of the frame, care being taken to get it into corners and low places, as if they had never been dusted. The luminall is then wiped away with cotton sheeting until the desired amount of antiquing remains. If the luminall has dried too much for easy handling, more may be applied to dampen the first coat and the excess wiped off. When the desired effect has been achieved, the frame is sprayed with clear lacquer. Japan may be used instead of luminall, but the latter is easier and creates a better effect.

SPATTER

This is a handsome way to tie a finish together. India ink is used—black, brown, rust red, and dark green are particularly effective. A brush with short stiff bristles is dipped into the ink and wiped on the side of the jar. Holding something like a 6-inch length of broom handle at about a 45-degree angle to the edge of the frame or mat, and the brush at right angles to the stick, the brush is tapped against the handle, causing delicate spots to fall on to the finished surface. Spatter should be applied quickly and evenly, and the ink should go straight down; if the ink "skids," the effect is lost. The first brushload should always be tested on a scrap of mat board or card-board, knocking off the extra ink with a firm tap so that a light tapping may be done on the finished surface. Practice will soon teach where the brush will send the spatter. The final coat is a clear lacquer spray.

STIPPLE

We use this as a finishing color touch to leafed fillets and mats, although, as with any other process, it can be applied to other uses, depending on the imagination of the finisher.

Cotton waste is soaked with ready-mixed alcohol dye and dabbed on in a somewhat random pattern, producing a brilliant color detail on top of gold or silver leaf. This procedure, using a walnut stain, creates a handsome antiquing on top of multicolored leaf, as on the mats we produce for icons and Christmas cards. A sponge may be used instead of cotton waste.

With the tools, materials, and processes just described, many more finishes are possible. Knowing what media are compatible and their effects when incompatible allows the extension into experimentation, which is what imag-inative finishing is all about.

9 SHADOW BOXES

CREATING a shadow box provides a refreshing and welcome change from routine framing. No area of framing is more taxing to the framer's imagination, ingenuity, and skill, but then nothing about his job is more fun, more rewarding, or more lucrative.

Webster's defines a shadow box as "a box, usually with a glass front, in which a framed painting may be kept to protect both painting and frame." As with most other dictionary definitions concerning picture framing (either absent, inadequate, or misleading), this hardly begins to describe what a shadow box really is. The parlance may vary among decorators and gift shop proprietors and even picture framers, but when we speak of a shadow box, we refer to a specially built frame consisting of various components, designed and constructed as a permanent housing for one or more three-dimensional objects.

Medals, coins, and plates are the most popular subjects for shadow boxes; however, anything that anyone wishes to take out of a drawer or from under the bed and hang on a wall can be successfully framed, whether it be a beaded bag from the Roaring Twenties, a cameo or brooch, a pair of golf clubs, a collection of cigarette lighters, or a full-sized pistol or sword. These in fact are only a few of the many objects we have been asked to frame. Others include a sprig of fresh edelweiss from a Swiss mountaintop; a child's violin and bow; a floral casket piece, circa 1800, fashioned of velvet flowers, leaves, and feathers; a glass tear bottle from a tomb in Istanbul; a collection of Chinese snuff bottles; groups of iron keys from Spain and Mexico; Ecuadorian dough dolls; jewelry, stitcheries, handkerchiefs, and scarves; matchbook covers; watches; and the trappings from a Knights Templar uniform excluding, fortunately, the plumed helmet; paper sculptures; ceramic animals; and even a Turkish shadow puppet made of dyed leather and boxed in such a way that it can be manipulated from outside the frame by strings controlling its movement. Obviously there is nothing standard about framing such unrelated objects, nor is there anything routine about even the simplest shadow box. Certain basic considerations, however, apply to every box we build.

A shadow box is intended to be highly decorative and eye-catching, and so it must combine elegance with flawless craftsmanship. Elegance is achieved by a judicious choice of fabric and color, and the arrangement of the objects being boxed. Craftsmanship brings up some highly technical considerations: how a three-dimensional object is to be attached to a background and how it is to be separated from the protecting glass. The customer is more interested in the type and color of fabric and the arrangement of his keepsakes, so the framer need not discuss engineering problems with him; in fact, in many cases he himself may not even know how such problems are to be solved until he gets into the actual work.

Basically a shadow box consists of a fabric-covered background, an optional decorative small gold or lacquered liner, a functional liner covered in the background fabric, and a frame that holds the glass. The size of the object, from front to back, determines the depth of the functional liner, which is usually a slant-in shape varying in width across the return from $3/4$ inch to $2\frac{1}{2}$ inches. If a deeper return is required, the inside of a frame may be lined; this involves covering upson board with fabric and gluing each section to the inside of the frame. (We have found it worth the expense to order a special run on a 6-inch deep stem moulding. This can accommodate almost any object that requires a shadow box, and can be ripped to a shallower depth if the full 6 inches isn't needed.)

Shadow box housing scholastic pins, baby ring, and heirloom jewelry. The beaded liner gives a touch of elegance. The shadow box is attached to a velvet-lined box by means of a piano hinge at the top. Both frames are gold leafed.

Assemblage by Gene Coe representing various aspects of the Mother Lode country. Three-quarter-inch liner covered in dark green velvet, six-inch shadow box stem lined in yellow velvet, stem frame in dark green stain.

Lining frames to create shadow boxes. 1. Two-and-a-half-inch frame. 2. Two-inch frame. 3. Velvet glued to front of lining. 4. Velvet turned and glued to back of lining.

The simplest type of shadow box is one that houses a tray or plate. Two inches of velvet is usually enough to show at top and sides (and the all-important extra $\frac{1}{2}$-inch at the bottom), particularly if the fabric is a strong color, like royal blue or red.* In the case of a $2\frac{1}{2}$-inch Viennese pin tray, the background is cut from upson board to $6\frac{1}{2}$ by 8 inches. The foot of the tray is measured and a circle scribed and cut, the circle being $\frac{1}{8}$ inch larger than the foot measurement since velvet is $\frac{1}{16}$ inch thick. The foot will fit snugly into the circle if this factor is kept in mind.

Velvet is laid to the top of the mat in the same manner that any fabric is applied, with the exception that more glue is used. Linen is laid when the glue is tacky. It should be thicker for velvet; the glue should be wetter for velvet. When the glue is set, the fabric is turned into the circular opening onto the back of the mat. Working from the back, pie-shaped wedges are cut, trimmed, and glued with hot glue. This background is glued to another of like size and the tray glued into the opening and slightly weighted until the glue has set.

111

* Since velvet is used more often than not for backgrounds and functional liners, we interchange the words velvet and fabric.

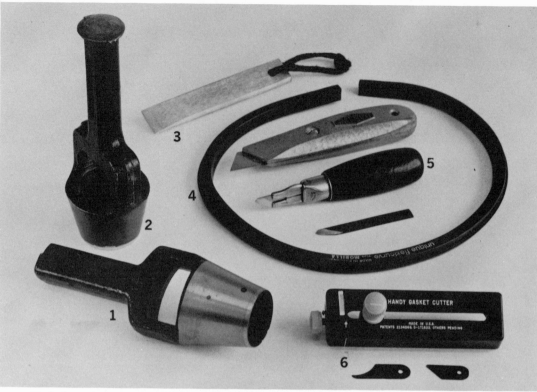

Tools for making circles. 1 and 2. Arch punches for stamping coin-sized holes. 3. Gerber's Sportsman's Steel for honing mat knives. 4. "Flexicurve," which may be curved to conform to irregular circles and ovals, so tracings may be made. 5. Mat knives and blade. 6. Gasket cutter with blades; may be adjusted to cut circles up to 6 inches.

Shadow box housing silver plate with engraved signatures. Frame hinged so it may be lifted and plate removed for cleaning.

Back view of shadow box for engraved silver plate. 1. Upson board background to which plate is attached with pressure-sensitive tape. 2. Background covered in velvet; upson board corners have been glued; first background will be glued to corners. 3. Functional liner covered in green velvet. 4. Walnut frame, glass.

Decorative liners. 1, 2, 3. Functional liners. 4, 7. (These are covered in fabric.) Frames 5, 6, 8.

The four sticks of functional liner are covered, following the same steps for covering any liner, but leaving an excess inch of fabric at each end. After the velvet has been trimmed from the back and from inside the rabbet, hot glue is applied to the end of the liner, which is turned into place. With good, dependable shears, a diagonal cut is made into the rabbet and the triangle of excess fabric snipped away. The two remaining tabs are then glued into the rabbet. The four corners are joined, and a velvet frame has been created.

"Teacart box" lined in royal blue velvet, silver leaf box and frame. Coins countersunk into blue velvet. Beaded decorative liner in silver leaf. Functional liner covered in blue velvet. Frame and hinge silver leafed. Box is 10 by 10½ inches and deep enough to hold dessert silverware.

If the circular saw is sharp, another technique may be used: the lengths of liner are cut about an inch longer than the required measurement, and the velvet laid. Working from the velvet side, the liner may be cut to correct size and joined. (This won't work on a chopper or with amateur equipment such as a hand saw or mitre box.)

Coins are countersunk in the same manner as the foot of the plate, with one notable exception: the circles need not be cut by hand because punches are available in coin sizes, and the holes may be hammered out. However, somewhat more skill is required in turning the fabric since all the work shows. Care should be taken that there are no overcuts.

Medals pose a bit more of a problem. While it would seem that they could be pinned to the background much as they are pinned to a uniform, the fact that the background is rigid makes this impossible; the hinge and clasp are bulky and cause the medal to tip off at an angle, and thus must be countersunk. With a mat knife and an awl, slits and holes should be cut into the covered background, and the hinge and clasp forced into the openings.

Objects that cannot be countersunk onto upson board backgrounds, such as dolls, bottles, or keys, need to be attached by other means and the fabric laid on a more porous background. Many three-dimensional objects may be hung by fine wire, by making a hole with an awl and threading the wire from the back, looping it around the object, forcing it back through the same hole, and tying securely. We have found that nylon fishing line, which is stronger than steel of the same weight and well-nigh invisible, is the most practical and durable material for attaching delicate subjects.

It isn't hard to convince a friendly veterinarian that his favorite picture framer won't poke his arm full of holes if he is provided with a 50-cc hypodermic syringe. The needle is inserted from the back, nylon fishline pushed through the needle's eye, and the needle withdrawn; it is then inserted from the front, and the line pushed through to join the other end. This loop may be tightened around the neck of a doll or the tail of a ceramic cat or the holes in a key, and we defy anyone to detect the manner in which the object is attached. A square knot is tied at the back, the needle acting as an extra set of fingers, and the knot secured by a small square of masking tape as extra reinforcement.

This procedure is useful in attaching flat objects as well: holding maps, tapestries, book pages, and scarves in place, where a nail or escutcheon pin would be too noticeable. The principal advantage is that it leaves no mark or hole on a fabric, particularly velvet, which is critical, since it uses only one thickness of thread. A sewing or darning needle cannot be trusted not to leave a hole—in fact, it can be trusted to leave a hole—not only because of its size but because it carries a double thickness of thread.

116

A most important consideration in designing a shadow box is to make the finished product look as logical as possible. Coins, jewelry, medals, and plates, simply countersunk, look perfectly at home. Dolls, artifacts, bottles, and statues, on the other hand, seem to be floating in space if they are simply attached to a background. They need some apparent support such as a pedestal, stand, or shelf even though the objects are attached to a background by wire or fishing line, as everything in a shadow box must be securely anchored. Objects we are used to seeing in a hanging position—a cup, a locket, a beaded bag—may be hung from an ornamental hook. Bottles may be lined up on a shelf; a sword or a gun may rest on ornamental brackets. Creating the illusion of a more natural setting is just one more trick the picture framer plays to make a wall hanging more pleasing to the eye.

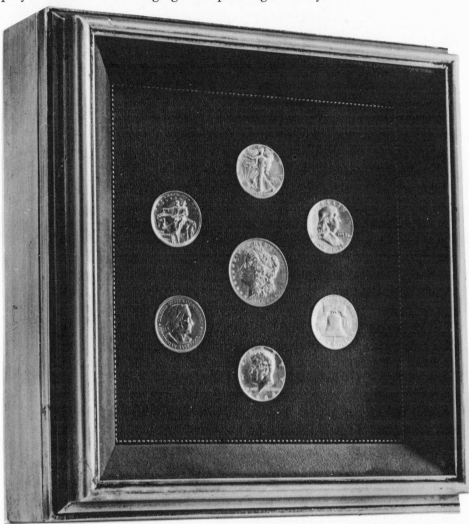

Shadow box on top of velvet-lined box that could hold dessert silver. The shadow box is attached to the box by means of a piano hinge, making it more secure than two regular hinges would be. Beaded decorative liner, velvet-covered functional liner, slant-back stem in silver leaf.

117

Balsa wood is easily carved to make a shelf or an ornamental bracket. A block of wood, sanded and lacquered or leafed, makes an adequate base. The shelf, base, or bracket can, with some imagination, be designed and finished to echo the origin of the subject—Oriental, baroque, Colonial, primitive, and the like. The bases may be attached from the back with a screw, or they may be glued into place.

Fitting a shadow box is painstaking and sometimes frustrating work. The fabric must be brushed entirely free of fish and, in the case of velvet, the nap brought up and made to run in one direction. As with all other fittings, the subject and components may seem to be entirely clean—until the glass goes on. A fitter might as well get used to the idea that a velvet-lined shadow box will have to be taken apart at least once. Velvet—particularly black—seems to have a magnetic quality when it comes to attracting bits of lint and other airborne nuisances. Patience, brushing, and even a lot of breath-holding go into this most delicate phase of the framer's work.

We cannot caution the amateur strongly enough to stay away from black velvet in his first attempts at building a shadow box. Black really isn't that effective, and there's no sense in foisting unnecessary frustrations on oneself. It is also to be mentioned that the framer doubles his fitting charges when black velvet is used.

Time after time we have encountered this situation: the customer has two or three or thirty items he would like to see in a shadow box, but he balks at the price. When asked for a breakdown of charges, he decides to save a few —or a hundred—dollars by doing his own fitting. It takes only a few days (or sometimes only a couple of hours) for him to come back, frustrated and apologetic, and suddenly with money in his pocket, with a better understanding of why he can no more do his own fitting than he can remove his own appendix or fill his own teeth.

It's hard to finish a book that really has no ending. Just as we think we have said it all, we remember another minuscule but important detail, find a new technique, try a new product, or discover another refinement in design.

We are reminded of a long-ago experience from which we emerged with an airtight, waterproof truism that applies to most areas of creativity: "If it can be defined, it's dead." A jazz trombonist of our acquaintance, teaching brass instrumentation at the university level, had finally been given the nod to create and deliver a series of lectures on jazz. He and a group of other musicians got together and tried to formulate a definition of jazz. After several lengthy, argumentative, and unproductive sessions, they still had no definition, even though the words spontaneous, creative, imaginative, and skillful kept cropping up. We kicked the idea around, off and on, comparing

Viennese pin tray (2½ inches in diameter) in velvet-lined shadow box. Upson board background covered in pale green velvet: ½-inch decorative gold liner with half round lip; ¾-inch functional liner covered in the stick with the background velvet; glass; prefinished gold stem frame. The functional liner serves to isolate the subject from the glass.

jazz to art, religion, teaching, learning, love—all the big words—and came to the realization that these are the areas of life that cannot be defined; in fact, anything that can be defined is immediately confined, doomed forever to unyielding rules. A wall of words may be put up around such objects as book, pencil, paintbrush, violin, but no such boundaries may be used to contain intangibles such as writing, drawing, painting, and music because there are no limits to be placed on creative skills.

Since we have put so much emphasis on the art of craftsmanship, we might revise that definition to include picture framing—and all the skills of other anonymous people we mentioned at the beginning: "If limits of creativity have been reached, it can't be called art." We have tried this on for size and find that it serves as a reverse truism as well: "Craftsmanship is art when no limits may be put on creativity."

APPENDIX I
Handling Special Problems

Ideally, an oil painting should be cleaned every ten years, which involves removing the old varnish and giving the canvas a coat of new varnish. An oil painting cannot be cleaned with Ivory soap and water. Water not only cannot dissolve varnish, but a big risk is taken that the unpainted canvas will get wet, causing permanent damage from mildew. In cleaning an oil painting, cotton waste soaked in alcohol is held in one hand, and cotton waste soaked in turpentine is held in the other. Alcohol is applied to a small area in a brisk circular motion, and at the proper moment, when the varnish has begun to "move," the action is stopped by applying turpentine in the same manner. The entire painting is cleaned in this way, and the process repeated if the varnish is particularly thick or dirty. It is not a job for amateurs.

Commercial cleaners for oil paintings are available, but here again the amateur should know what he is doing and why before he embarks upon a massive refurbishing of the family's oils. It's a good idea to become familiar with the action of the solution, through practice and experimentation. It is also to be kept in mind that more and more paintings are being done in mixed media, and that a cleaning solution could be used safely on one medium while it might work catastrophe on another.

The life-span and efficiency of a glass-cutting tool may be prolonged if it is kept in a small jar containing kerosene. A glass cutter is sharpened by placing the wheel against the beveled edge of a piece of Arkansas slipstone, rolling the cutter back and forth, then turning to the other side and repeating. Each fitter likes to have his own glass cutter, used only by him, as the tool adjusts to his touch in the same way a mat knife does.

Occasionally we find a piece of breath-blown glass on an old picture that we are reframing or refurbishing. Before glass was manufactured by modern methods, a glass blower first blew a cylinder, then split it and allowed it to flatten in an annealing oven, resulting in the flattest piece of glass he could achieve, but not flat as we know it today. Breath-blown glass has a "wivvery" look, echoing the days of handcrafting. When a customer learns that he owns such a rarity, he usually follows our suggestion to have it silvered, to use as a mirror. With a velvet liner and an elaborate frame, it becomes a pleasant wall hanging and conversation piece, even though it is hardly functional as a mirror.

It goes without saying, but we frequently have to say it: no work can be done on a picture or a frame without removing the picture from the frame, and many are the messes we have cleaned up because some earnest handyman either didn't know this or chose not to believe it.

When framing a mirror, one should be sure to give the rabbet a coat of black paint to avoid a reflection of raw wood around the edges of the mirror. This is true even if there is a fabric-covered liner; while the rabbet is not reflected around the edges, the raw corners tend to show.

If one has occasion to move or ship a glazed picture, it is well to remember that glass bends before it breaks. Masking tape applied diagonally across the face of the glass at two- or three-inch intervals, and in both directions, will absorb much of the shock and prevent considerable breakage. This trick is particularly successful when one is doing one's own moving, but is not an absolute guarantee when pictures are being shipped by public carrier.

A grease spot can be removed from a mat by taking it out of the frame, touching the spot with a dollop of benzine, and setting it in bright sunlight for a few minutes. The process may have to be repeated several times, but if the spot is grease, it eventually will lift off, leaving no ring.

122

Grilled cheese sandwiches can be made in the dry-mount press with only a minor adaptation, but if it is at all convenient, we suggest going out for lunch.

One of the oldest, cheapest, and most effective of all adhesives is plain wallpaper paste or wheat paste. This can be made from wheat flour mixed with cold water and heated until it thickens. (Shades of rainy Saturdays in one's childhood!) For all practical purposes, however, it is easier to buy a non-staining wheat paperhangers' paste at the hardware store, already mixed and cooked and ready to use.

The trim rollers used to spread white glue can be used longer, more efficiently, and more economically if they are properly stored. Plastic sandwich bags make ideal receptacles. The roller is encased in a bag so that it touches the inside of the bag only at the handle. A rubber band is used to close the top of the bag around the handle, keeping the bag airtight and the glue wet, and the roller hung on a nail or cuphook. This saves time, and glue that would have been washed away is preserved.

Crumpled currency can be restored to mint condition if wetted and placed in the dry-mount press under light heat.

A dry-mount film known as Fotoflat is available for mounting papers that may need to be removed from the mount board at a future time. This product is particularly useful for mounting watercolors, which tend to present an irregular look that many people object to. Mounting, of course, corrects such irregularities, but a watercolor is a piece of original art whose intrinsic value is destroyed by mounting. Application of heat makes it possible to unmount the watercolor from Fotoflat in case the picture increases in value and is sent back to the marketplace.

Sooner or later, bits of film, paper, and other foreign matter get stuck to the platen of the dry-mount press. If not removed, these can severely damage subjects being mounted. The platen may be unscrewed from the press and cleaned with a rough-textured nylon cloth known as a 3-M scrubber, available in most hardware stores. Stubborn specks may be further worked out with a fiber glass eraser.

Wallpaper paste deteriorates quickly if left exposed to the air; mold and mildew begin to appear within 24 hours if the container is not tightly closed. A life expectancy of at least a week is assured when a pot of paste is stored thus: a container is created by cutting the tops from two empty plastic jugs just below the taper of the neck (one-gallon white glue jugs are excellent; the plastic containers for fruit juice make handy one-quart storage). The bottom container makes an ideal mixing tub, and the tapered bottom of the second may be fitted into the top of the first, assuring an airtight condition. The lid, then, also serves as a convenient holder for upended brushes.

123

A mold-proof, presized, non-staining fortified wheat paste has recently come onto the market. Called Shur-Stik, it is available at good hardware stores.

Rice flour paste has fine adhesive qualities, dries clear and free from any yellow color, and is recommended for mounting thin, delicate, almost transparent papers and fabrics, or pieces that have suffered heavy damage, such as old documents, or photos that have been rolled, newspapers, and subjects that may have lost parts of their borders during the aging process. Rice flour is obtainable in any store handling Oriental food, and is mixed in exactly the same way that wallpaper paste is made except not boiled, just heated until it thickens. The mounting technique is also the same, but a finer brush is used, such as sable or ox hair, and somewhat more time and patience are required, since the subject is usually delicate. Rice flour is a handy item to keep on the kitchen shelf, making an elegant breading for shrimps and other deep-fried food.

Once in a while a mounting job involves two or more pieces that need to be laid side by side with butted joints, such as a triptych, sections of a chart, two pages from a book, or additions to a map. As a rule the components do not represent a perfect fit. To correct this discrepancy the two papers are laid side by side, allowing an overlap of no more than $\frac{1}{16}$ inch, a heavy steel rule is laid directly on top of the lapped joint, and, with a good razor blade, a cut is made through both thicknesses of paper, creating a perfect joint.

If the occasion arises to buy salvage plate glass, it is good thinking to pay a nominal extra charge for having the edges seamed (ground but not polished), which saves a lot of bloodletting in ultimate handling.

All too often we encounter original graphics that have been badly damaged through careless storage, broken glass, or improper shipping. These can be restored by the wet-mounting technique, using only water as they should not be mounted. The process is simple, requiring only patience and adequate workspace. Two pieces of plate glass, larger than the print, are thoroughly cleaned and one generously wetted with tap water. The subject is placed face down on the wet glass and wetted with a clean sponge—in fact, soaked—so that it is stretched flat, held to the glass by the surface tension of the water. Using absorbent papers (those from boxed glass are good) as much moisture as possible is removed, drawing the water from the print. When the absorbent paper no longer laps up extra water, the print is covered with several layers of dry absorbent paper and covered with the second piece of plate glass. After twelve to twenty-four hours, the top glass is removed and the papers, quite wet by now, are replaced with new, dry paper, and the pressing process is repeated.

When no ripples appear in the covering papers (two or three repetitions later), the top glass is set directly onto the subject and all of it set into direct sunlight. Steam and mist will form on the glass, indicating that the piece is still damp, but as soon as these elements no longer manifest themselves, the print is entirely dry and has been restored to mint condition.

When it is necessary to remove a temporarily mounted subject from a background—a photograph or a calendar print, for instance, that has been mounted to cardboard or paper with a dollop of rubber cement at each corner—surer success can be expected if the subject is placed face down and the background removed. This places the stress of pulling on the background rather than on the subject. The ideal tool in this case is an English bone, a bookbinder's tool made of polished bone, 1 inch wide and 9 inches long, lightly pointed at each end, and available at good stationery or art-supply stores. The bone is gently eased across the bonded surface while the background is pulled away. Another method of quick removal is this: the subject is weighted under a heavy steel rule and the background paper is rolled onto a mailing tube.

Should the occasion arise—and it has!—that candle wax needs to be removed from fabric, the soluble agent is amyl acetate, commonly known as banana oil. The usual source is a good drugstore, but we found that, at least in Los Angeles, shelf storage of this product has been prohibited under certain anti-pollution laws; our source, therefore, is a manufacturing chemist.

Scotch tape, one of the deadliest enemies known to paper, may be removed by the careful use of methyl ethyl ketone. Success is not always assured, as certain discolorations caused by the tape are sometimes all too permanent.

To restore a foxed etching or engraving, one must have an area in which he can work with lots of water. A bench covered with a large piece of plate glass will do, or a bathtub if the subject is oversized.

The engraving is first soaked with enough water to hold it to a sheet of plate glass by surface tension. Next it is flooded with a dilute solution of ammonium carbonate (crystals dissolved in water) and flooded with fresh water until no odor remains.

Next it is flooded with a dilute solution of white vinegar, and washed again with clear water until no odor remains. (Sometimes it is advisable to turn the paper over at this point and work from the other side.)

Now it is flooded with a weak solution of sodium hypochlorate (household bleach) and again washed until no odor remains.

If all spots have not disappeared, the process is repeated. All the washes should be running under the paper; if they are not, it is necessary to turn it over frequently so that both sides will be treated. It is advisable to handle the wet paper by clamping it between two pieces of mat board rather than to try to lift it with the fingers.

After the final washing, the subject is covered with another piece of plate glass and the "sandwich" set out in full sunlight. As the paper begins to dry, the glass will fog. The top glass should be removed and replaced by another piece of glass. The first glass is cleaned and dried to be kept ready for the next replacement. This process of replacing fogged glass is repeated until no fogging occurs. At this point the sandwich is brought inside and allowed to dry—from two days to a week. In addition to drying time, the process takes about an hour, give or take a little, depending on one's dexterity.

The restored subject should be matted and backed by 100 percent rag paper.

"Butter paper," a favorite with amateur and professional artists for sketching, is the framer's headache. The only adhesive to use with it, if mount one must, is rice flour paste.

Occasionally, after a print or map has been mounted and leaves the store, a bubble may appear—either because of atmospheric conditions or because of a quality in the paper or the glue. Whatever the reason, some place along the line, the mount board is no longer forming a perfect union with the print, and the framer must correct it. First we try applying low heat with a warm iron, protecting the print with a piece of paper. If this doesn't work, we take a deep breath and embark on a more complicated process, which attacks the problem from the back of the print, and with that same old handy hypodermic syringe.

First the bubble is located and carefully marked on the back of the mounting board. Three holes are then made within the marked area, using a nail or the hypodermic needle. One hole is for shooting glue into the bubble, the other two for letting out the air that is causing the bubble. Now glue is diluted with water to make a free-flowing liquid, poured into the syringe, and the needle inserted through the mount board and glue shot into the bubble. When the diluted glue flows freely out of the two air holes, the subject is placed on edge to allow the glue to flow to the edge of the bubble. The subject should be turned to the second, third, and fourth sides for two or three minutes each. The print is then placed flat, face up, and the bubble may be pressed away with the fingers. The subject is covered with glass, weighted, and allowed to dry at least overnight.

126

This process can be applied to mounted oil paintings that have buckled with time.

To cut a mat out of square, a sheet of architect's tracing paper is placed on the face of the subject and the corners marked with soft pencil. The tracing paper is then placed face down on the back of mat board and the soft-penciled lines marked with a hard pencil. Lines are scribed against these markings and the mat cut in the usual fashion.

While there is nothing really new about the three-dimensional (3-D) or "floating" frame, it is still considered one of the most contemporary shapes we use. It almost invariably * must be used with a liner because there is no rabbet, and obviously the liner must be covered around the edges instead of being trimmed. (Or lacquer sprayed all over instead of just on the face.) The easiest way to fit a liner into a 3-D frame is this: an appropriate number of screw eyes, depending on the size of the frame, are attached to the inside of the frame, then 3/4- or 1-inch screws are dropped through the eyes and attached to the back of the liner.

If a print has been rolled for some time and still retains that recalcitrant shape, it may be handled more easily if, before mounting, it is rolled in reverse on a length of kraft paper and taped. The next day—or even within a couple of hours—the print will lie flat when unrolled.

Frames for 8- by 10-inch or 11- by 14-inch photographs usually have to be cut to 7½ by 9½ and 10½ by 13. The paper size is 8 by 10 or 11 by 14, but if the frame is not cut to the smaller dimension, the white edge will show around the photograph. It is wise not to take phone orders unless this point of measurement has been discussed.

As a commentary on human behavior, we have noticed that a customer will spot an infinitesimal flaw on a frame or mat surrounding a photograph of his wife or child, but the same flaw goes unnoticed if the picture is of himself. The same holds true if the subject is a diploma, a citation signed by a dignitary, or a significant award. Before we take a job apart to remove a small fish, we consider the vanity aspects.

Stark white paper may be antiqued in several ways. If it is a document signed in ink, or if it has any other property that might be damaged with wetting, it can be "cooked" either in an oven or in the dry-mount press. Three

---

* *Almost invariably is qualified by occasional instances when a subject can be mounted to a wooden background. The edges of the board are painted, and the background is attached to the frame as if it were a liner.*

hundred degrees is about right; the length of cooking time depends on the thickness of the paper and the amount of antiquing that is desired. A black and white print (a brass rubbing comes to mind) may be either dipped in or sponged with a solution of tea, then flecked with cigarette tobacco while the piece is still damp. If the subject has been lacquered, it can be antiqued by rubbing on a mixture made of rottenstone suspended in liquid wax.

To clean photographs that have collected years of dust (and until recently we have told customers that there isn't much we can do with photographs), Amway's LOC in water, applied with velvet in a circular motion, has been unusually successful. This technique is also apparently useful in removing Scotch tape. The solution should be allowed to work for about a minute after application, and then it may be wiped away with the scrap of dampened velvet, lifting years of dirt and grime. Scotch tape will have to be nudged with a razor blade in most instances.

A Japanese calligraphy brush, or any other brush whose shape is important, should be washed in soap and water and then impregnated with clean wet soap and hung to dry. This holds the bristles together and helps to maintain the important shape of the brush.

Every framer has encountered the almost daily experience of designing and pricing a frame for, say, a photograph, only to be asked by the customer, "Now, will that have a little stand on the back so I can set the picture on a table?" The answer, of course, is yes—at a substantially higher charge. "Why should that be extra?" asks the customer. This is why:

To build an easelback we first cut a piece of mat board to a size just smaller than the outside measurements of the frame. (How much smaller is determined by the thickness of the fabric with which it is to be covered.) A wedge is next cut from mat board, representing the leg the easel is to stand on. Next a slit is cut in the rectangular mat board, just long enough for the end of the wedge to slide through. (If the picture is to be used alternately on a table and hanging on a wall, it is advisable to cut the rectangle out of double-thick mat board and to cut out the contour of the wedge, to make the "leg" fit flush into the back of the easel.

Next the mat board is covered in fabric: the fabric is glued to the face of the board and turned, mitering the corners. A length of narrow grosgrain ribbon, or a piece of shoelace, is cut and pulled through a hole made at the lower center of the wedge, just long enough to provide a tab that can be glued down. The wedge is then covered on one side with matching fabric. About an inch of the wedge is folded down at the top, slipped through the slit in the mat board, and secured with hot glue.

128

The uncovered side of the wedge is backed with kraft paper, as a picture is backed. The other end of the ribbon is slipped through the mat board and drawn to the proper length to allow the easelback to stand comfortably. Excess ribbon is cut off and the tab glued down.

The easelback is then attached to the back of the frame with tiny brass escutcheon pins, as many as necessary according to the size of the finished picture.

Quite an adequate easelback may be made by cutting a lopsided pentagon from mat board. First a rectangle is cut (size to be determined by the size of the frame), a pencil line is drawn down the middle from top to bottom, the long side lopped off on the paper cutter at an angle, and another angle cut off from center bottom to the edge of the first angle. Mystic tape is applied, and the board is scored at the marked center. The rectangular part of the board is attached with hot glue to the back of the fitted frame and weighted until dry. The irregularly cut wedge serves as the stand.

APPENDIX II
Building a Carton

To build the eggcrate carton is to build the ego! To construct a box that not only resists but defies what seems to be malicious mishandling and deliberate brutalizing by the public carriers produces a sense of smug satisfaction amounting to pure euphoria.* Never again the time-consuming and frustrating attempts to collect insurance if the box is broken and the contents damaged. Never again having to label a package *Fragile* and *Handle with Care*, for the simple reason that the eggcrate carton is not fragile and need not be handled with care. Moreover, we know of no more economical way of shipping a package since charges amount to the weight of a piece of double-faced corrugated board plus the weight of the subject.

Material and tools are minimal: a sheet of double-faced corrugated board, a few feet of gummed kraft tape, measuring tape, steel rule, mat knife, and a good sense of precision.

130

* *Postal authorities will readily admit that any package going through the U.S. mails should be wrapped with the expectation that it will be jumped on by a 150-pound employee.*

The purpose of the box is to surround the framed picture (or other object) by two inches of air. It consists of seven pieces: the master box, two dummy boxes, and four notched inserts for holding the dummies in position within the master box.

We are taking as an example a framed picture measuring $8\frac{1}{2}$ by 11 inches. If a build-along is being considered at this point, it need not be a practice session or a trial run, as any measurements may be substituted for our three original measurements, the other calculations remaining the same.

Double-faced corrugated board for the master box is cut to size $17\frac{1}{2}$ by 55, that dimension having been reached in this manner:

$8\frac{1}{2}$	11	$\frac{1}{2}$	(or substitutions)
$+4$	$+4$	$+4\frac{1}{2}$	The 4-inch measurements represent the 2 inches of air around the dummy boxes; the
$12\frac{1}{2}$	15	5	$4\frac{1}{2}$ inches will be a fold-in flap.
$+5$			This is the second depth dimension.
$17\frac{1}{2}$			Width of board.
$12\frac{1}{2}$	(above) 15		
$12\frac{1}{2}$	15		
25	$+$	$30 = 55$ Length of board.	

The board is now measured, marked, and scored at $12\frac{1}{2}$, 15, and $12\frac{1}{2}$ across its width. Scoring, breaking—no, bending—the surface of the top layer of corrugated board is done with the blunt end of a pair of shears against a steel rule.

Next the length of the board is scored at $6\frac{1}{4}$—half of $12\frac{1}{2}$ (or whatever that number is up there, at the first addition), measuring from the outside edges toward the center, from the center dimension. Eight slits are cut at the $12\frac{1}{2}$-inch measurement and $\frac{1}{4}$ inch of board removed. This step frees the flaps that become the top and bottom of the box; the size of the short measurement is reduced by $\frac{1}{2}$ inch (two times the $\frac{1}{4}$ inch) to allow for an exact fit with no overlap when the box is assembled.

The eggcrate sections are made by cutting four pieces of board to the first dimensions of the box: $12\frac{1}{2}$ by 15 by 5 inches. These are notched to the dimension of the subject: $8\frac{1}{2}$ by 11 inches.

The two dummy boxes are made of two pieces of board measured to $12\frac{1}{2}$ by 15 inches. These are scored at 2 inches from the sides, four times each to make a corner. Squares are cut out at the four corners and the sides folded in. The corners are sealed with kraft tape to form a topless box.

The box is assembled by folding the length at the three scored marks and sealing the ends with gummed tape. The bottom flaps are folded in and the bottom sealed. The eggcrates are locked and set into the box. One dummy is

131

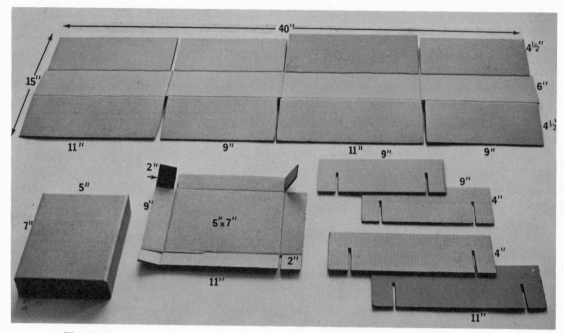

The finished dummy box, bottom up. Dummy box before folding and taping. Eggcrate sections before assembling.

For a 5-by-7-by-2-inch picture, the dimensions would be figured thus:

$$\begin{array}{lll} 5'' & 7'' & 2'' \\ +\ 4'' & +\ 4'' & +4\tfrac{1}{2}'' \\ \hline 9'' & 11'' & 6\tfrac{1}{2}'' \\ +\ 6\tfrac{1}{2}'' & & \\ \hline 15\tfrac{1}{2}'' & & \end{array}$$

(representing 2″ of air all around $+\tfrac{1}{2}$″ overlap)

(9″ is width of box; 11″ is length; 6½″ is depth)

(width of board to be cut for outside box)

$$\begin{array}{ll} 15\tfrac{1}{2}'' & 18'' \\ +15\tfrac{1}{2}'' & +18'' \\ \hline 31'' & +36'' \end{array}$$

length 67″

2 times 9 + 2 times 11 = 40, length of board for outside box

Outside dimensions of dummy boxes are 9″ by 11″ (to be reduced to 5″ by 7″ when two inches are scored and folded to make a box). Eggcrate sections are cut to 9″ by 11″ by 4″, and notched (to the inside) at 2″.

Scoring is done on the large piece—the box proper—at 4½″ from the outsides, on the long length; at 11″ and 9″ and 11″ in that order from the left side of the 40″ length. Scoring is done at 5″ and 7″ on the dummy boxes.

Notches are cut ¼″ wide toward the outside of the scorings on dummy boxes; alternating on box proper, to allow for exact fit.

set in, open end down. The subject—it need not be wrapped—is nestled into place, and the second dummy box is set in, open side up. Gummed tape is applied to the 2-inch loose flap inside the top dummy, and extended over and down into the eggcrate, creating a rigid and jolt-resisting buffer.

132

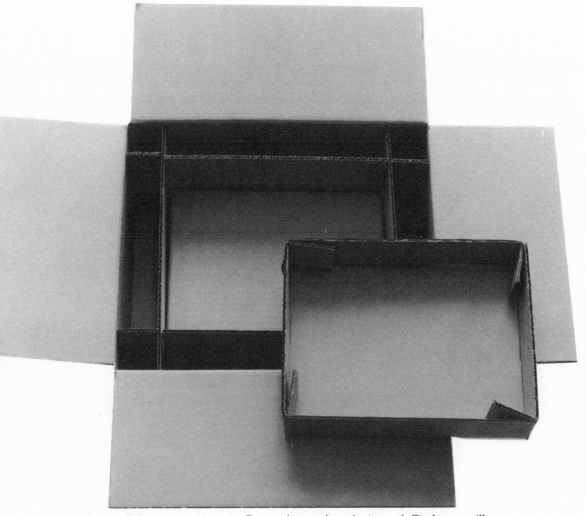

Assembled box before picture is put in. Dummy box ready to be inserted. Final steps will be taping and addressing.

A box of any dimension may be made from these instructions. Double-faced corrugated board is available in a maximum size of 36 by 72 inches; however, larger sheets may be made by butting two sheets together and sealing both sides with kraft tape.

It is to be noted that the carton need not be wrapped. Sealed across the top, it is adequately protected for handling by any type of carrier.

And the reason we cannot patent it is that we have used it for seven years, which is six years past the deadline. We take satisfaction, however, in being able to say that we have shipped cartons of all sizes all over the United States and the world, and have never had reports of any damage.

GLOSSARY

ACRYLIC

A water-based plastic paint that comes in a myriad of colors, in tubes or jars, to be used with brushes or a palette knife. It may be thinned with water to be used as watercolor, or taken directly from the tube and used as oil paint. If mixed with a gloss polymer medium, it attains a high glaze. A completely permanent paint.

AMYL ACETATE

Banana oil. Useful as a solvent for spot-cleaning fabrics.

ANTIQUING

Anything the framer does to make something look old; to produce an artificial patina whether it be a new print, a map, a leafed mat, or a frame. (Antiquing of prints is discussed in the Appendix; antiquing mat and frame in the chapter on finishing.)

BEVEL

The angle at which a mat is cut; inside—toward the picture, or reverse—away from the picture.

BORGHESE (bor-gay-see)

Refers both to a moulding shape within the trade, and to a finish for mats, fillets, and frames (silver leaf washed with raw sienna in japan).

BURNISHER

An agate-tipped pencil-like tool most commonly used in burnishing leaf, but also useful for smoothing paper when an erasure has roughened the surface, and for transferring ready-made lettering from its tissue to a mat.

COMPO

A mixture of Belgian whiting and glue that is moulded and fixed onto a frame by its own glue to create ornamental corners, an overall decoration, or a running bead. While compo usually takes a leafed finish, it can also be lacquered. Unfinished it looks much like raw cookie dough. There are innumerable patterns, and details can also be transferred from existing patterns. Many shops lay their own compo; we send ours out to a company that does nothing else.

COUNTERMOUNT

The application of paper to the back of a mounted subject. (See wet mounting.)

CRABS

Bits of lint and dirt that plague the fitter by getting between the subject and glass. Also called fish.

DRY MOUNT

One method of attaching a photograph, print, or certificate to a firmer background for better appearance and easier handling. The process involves heat and plastic film, using an electric iron or a dry-mount press.

DYKES

Diagonal pliers used for cutting wire and for removing tack points and brads when a picture is taken apart for reframing.

EPOXY

A double-action adhesive used when the strongest possible bond is needed between subject and background, such as a three-dimensional object in a shadow box.

FACE TO FACE AND BACK TO BACK

This catchy little phrase should always be remembered when two or more pictures are being transported from one place to another. Pictures should be stacked frame facing frame and screw eyes facing screw eyes. This is to prevent the screw eyes on the back of one picture from gouging into the frame on the next one. Screw eyes can easily work their way through even a protective piece of double-face corrugated board; sometimes it is wise, when stacking pictures of different sizes face to face, to insert a piece of corrugated or mat board to prevent one frame from scratching the glass on the next picture.

FILLET

A second mat under the first mat, of contrasting color or in metal leaf. Its sole purpose is decorative. The fillet may be cut from colored mat board or lacquered; occasionally it may be decorated with a small compo running detail. Double fillets, of two contrasting colors, are particularly effective in some circumstances.

135

FINISHING

The ultimate treatment of raw wood whether at the factory or in the frame shop. Many shops, because of zoning laws or lack of equipment, depend entirely upon prefinished moulding; others use only raw wood and do all their own finishing; still others, such as we, use a combination of both, customizing factory-finished mouldings by adding color, antiquing, or spatter.

FISH

Bits of lint and dirt that plague the fitter by getting between the subject and glass. Also called crabs.

FITTING

Putting the picture together with its components. Also called assembling. Score another one for anonymity: the insurance companies have no category for picture framers; we are insured under "furniture assembling."

FOXING

To discolor with yellowish-brown stains, as prints, book leaves, etc. Superficial stains are due to dampness and fungus; deeper stains to rusting of bits of iron in the paper. Foxing also occurs if an unmounted picture is backed directly by paper or corrugated board with a sulphur content. Foxed etchings or engravings may be restored by a process described in the Appendix.

FRENCH VARNISH

Sometimes called French polish, this is a highly refined byproduct of white shellac. French varnish is used to secure gold leaf to frames and mats—as well as to furniture —before the final coat of bar top lacquer is applied. (If French varnish is not applied, the leaf is inclined to lift when only bar top is used.) The traditional way to produce French varnish is to place a gallon jug of white shellac in direct sunlight. After two or three months, a white mass of resin settles to the bottom of the jug while a clear amber liquid rises to the surface. This is drawn off and used as French varnish. No use has been found for the white residue, so this process results in considerable waste; however, it will hardly disturb the economy, as French varnish is used in infinitesimal amounts and goes a long way.

Zehrung Chemical Company manufactures (in the Los Angeles plant) a fine quality shellac from which most of the wax has been removed. This can be thinned with alcohol, resulting in a fast-drying, water-thin, indispensable product. (The label refers to the product as Eight-Pound Cut, which means that eight pounds of refined shellac are held in suspension in a gallon of liquid.)

GAS SAND

The finest emery cloth is impregnated with gasoline, benzine, or even water and used as a polishing device when an absolutely glasslike surface is desired. While this process is used most frequently on lacquer finishes and to prepare a surface for leafing, it is also effective on wood.

GLASS

Two kinds are used: single-strength regular glass and non-reflecting (also called non-glare, Trusite, Silksite, depending on the manufacturer). Picture glass is thinner than window glass, each box containing 50 square feet up to size 32 by 40 inches. Glass is listed by manufacturers as containing so many lights (or panes) per box. For example a box of 22 x 28 glass contains 12 lights. Larger sizes are boxed at 100 square feet. Glass manufacturers have determined what sizes are most practical for economical use by framers, and stock-sized frames are determined by the sizes of stock-sized glass—8 by 10, 9 by 12, 11 by 14, 12 by 16, etc.

GLASS ERASER

An abrasive brush made of fiber glass, it is ideal for cleaning metal (the bottom of an iron, the platen in a dry-mount press) and for removing stubborn spots from mat board or linen.

HOT GLUE

Flakes made from animal hooves and hides, dissolved in cold water and then heated to produce an ideal adhesive for turning fabric mats and liners, and for backing pictures in the final state of fitting.

JAPAN

A clear, fast-drying varnish into which color can be dissolved to be used as a toning agent over metal leaf finishes. It is soluble in turpentine, paint thinner, gasoline, and benzine.

JEWELERS' ROUGE

An invaluable abrasive and burnishing compound for polishing coins, engraved plates, and other metal objects the framer might be asked to handle. Dark red in color, it comes in a brick or in a stick resembling an oversized crayon, and is applied by impregnating a cloth with benzine, rubbing the rouge from the stick. Patient polishing results in a high gloss as well as the removal of many flaws and scratches. Available at good hardware stores. One stick should last a lifetime unless one has an obsession about polishing metal.

KIOBE CORNERS

Special treatment on the corners of a raw frame to create an Oriental effect. (Described in the chapter on cut-and-join.)

LINER

A wooden frame as narrow as 3/8-inch finished in leaf or lacquer, and as wide as 6 inches, covered with fabric. Liners are used as a separation between a painting and a frame, or as an insert as an extra decorative touch.

MAT

Mats are cut from mat board, double-thick mat board, and upson board, with a window opening to show the picture. Used on watercolors, graphics, pastels, photographs, certificates, and citations—anything printed on paper.

MITRE

The angle on which the frame is cut. By varying the angle of the mitre, the framer can make octagonal, hexagonal, triangular or diamond-shaped frames.

MOUNT AND LACQUER

Attaching a subject to a background to remove wrinkles or fold marks, for easier handling and a professional look; then spraying with clear lacquer as a protection against dirt, dust, smoke, light, and grease. Lacquering in no way changes the colors in a print, and it affords as much protection as glass.

137

MYLAR

A transparent film that is applied to photographs, drawings, and papers to protect them from dirt, wear, and aging. It is applied with heat and pressure (a dry-mount press or electric iron). It resists water, grease, and oxidization, and protects against tearing and wear. It is completely transparent and adheres permanently. Particularly useful when both sides of a subject need to be seen (as book pages) and the weight of two pieces of glass is a factor.
(Seal-Lamin Laminating Film, Seal Incorporated, Derby, Connecticut.)

NAIL PULLER

A useful tool for opening boxes of glass. It has two jaws that close on either side of a nail head, and a lever that permits lifting the nail, minimizing glass breakage.

OVALS AND CIRCLE FRAMES

Custom construction is limited to a small number of frame shops. Most are manufactured in Europe and handled through moulding companies.

PRECOVERED LINERS

Lengths of moulding that have been covered in the stick at the factory so it need only be cut and joined. This molding can be purhased in linen and velvet, with or without a gold-leaf lip. Advantage: money-saver; disadvantage: it is usually too narrow for any but small paintings, and the joined corners show and sometimes even ravel, detracting from what could be a professional job.

PREFINISHED MOULDINGS

Any number of factories across the United States and Europe produce leafed, lacquered, driftwooded, distressed, and otherwise finished mouldings that need only be cut and joined and touched up at the corners. Some shops use only prefinished mouldings, others use only raw mouldings that are finished in the shop, and many, such as we, use a combination of both.

PRESSURE SENSITIVE TAPE

This is also called double-faced tape, as it is impregnated with adhesive on both sides. Useful for adhering pictures to mats or mats to mats when the permanence of glue is undesirable.

RABBET

The space inside the back of the frame where the picture, and the glass, if used, fits. A rabbet measurement is taken from the back of a frame, from rabbet edge to rabbet edge. When a frame is described as 16 by 20, the rabbet measurement is inferred, as opposed to a "sight" measurement, which see.

ROUNDED CORNERS

The raw frame is filed at the corners before finishing, producing a round look instead of square. This is only used when a decorator has a notion of doing something different.

SAWTOOTH HANGER

An aluminum hanging device, with notches on the lower edge and nail holes at either end, affixed to the top center of the frame (or two to a side if the frame is large.) Advantages: allows for flatter hanging, and for simple refitting when pictures are interchanged in one frame, as the more cumbersome screw eyes and wire are eliminated.

SCREW EYES AND WIRE

The usual device for hanging pictures. Screw eyes come in a wide assortment of sizes and are selected at the fitting table according to the weight of the picture.

SIGHT MEASUREMENT

This measurement is taken from the edges of a picture as seen from the front, and is used when the intention is to see all the picture to the edge of the paper it is printed on.

SPONGES

Three or four clean sponges should be kept around the worktable. Heavily wetted, they serve to dampen work that needs to be stretched; wrung as dry as possible, a sponge may be used to clean such hard-to-clean spots as those on photographs, serigraphs, and lacquered prints. If a dampened sponge is used on a newly mounted print before it is rolled with the brayer, surface dirt and excess paste are removed and the brayer kept clean.

STRETCHER BARS

These are wooden sections with two notches in each end that are fitted into each other and the four sides squared. The canvas is then stretched and stapled to the stretcher bars and two wooden keys are pounded into each corner, providing a completely taut surface. These may also be used to stretch stitcheries and tapestries.

STRIPPING (BATTEN)

Straight-sided wood with no rabbet, available at lumberyards if an artist wants to do his own framing. This is a great money-saver as the moulding is simply nailed to the sides of a stretched canvas. (No liner, no fitting to speak of.) Gold- or silver-topped stripping, cut on a mitre and joined, makes a handsome minimal frame, particularly on contemporary paintings or as temporary framing for a show.

TACK-POINT GUN

An indispensable tool for the framer, a useful one for artists who do their own framing and fitting. This falls generally into the category of a stapling machine, but shoots, with some force, diamond-shaped metal points into the inside edge of the frame, saving much time in nailing.

TALCUM POWDER

When the finest possible abrasive is needed for final burnishing on metal, ordinary shaving talcum is the ideal product, and the heel of the hand the ideal applicator.

TEMLOCK

A refined wood pulp wallboard used for mounting. It is $3/8$ inch thick, and porous enough to receive pins and thumbtacks for maps and bulletin boards.

TITANATED SHELLAC

Clear shellac with titanium white pigment added. A superlative wood sealer, it is easy to apply, fast drying, and provides a mirror-smooth surface as an undercoat for gold leaf or lacquer finishes.

TURNBUTTONS AND SCREWS

139

Metal devices of various sizes with a hole in one end allowing for attachment to the back of a frame by a small screw. At right-angle position, half a dozen turnbuttons hold the glass, mat, subject, and backing into the frame. Manipulated back into the parallel position, they allow for easy removal and interchange of subject, eliminating professional fitting and backing. This is of particular help to schools, where children's artwork is changed from week to week; it is also helpful to the collector who may want to rotate a set of prints.

UPSON BOARD

Mounting board, $\frac{3}{16}$-inch thick, nonporous, and helpfully rigid, this product makes a grand backing for posters, maps, photographs, and the like, as the outside edge can be cut on a bevel, creating a surface that accepts colored acrylics; the color acts as the finishing touch so the subject need not be framed.

WEIGHTS

All manner of weights are used for holding a subject down while it dries or is in some other process of handling. Large sheets of plate glass are used for pressing mounted prints. Small (4 by 4 inches) packages of stacked glass scraps wrapped in kraft paper make good weights for holding small objects in place to dry. A wrapped brick provides a good weight, as do a stack of printer's metal slugs. For weighting three-dimensional objects, such as plastic relief maps, a bag of sand is useful, as it adjusts to the contours of the subject.

INDEX

All *italic* figures refer to illustrations.